"I am delighted to recommend this book by my colleague Joe Boot. He gently urges his readers to consider the 'big questions of life,' for indeed, as he shows us, they are inescapable. And who more fitting to guide us through these questions than a young man with a passion and vision for our world rooted in his love for God?"

—DR. RAVI ZACHARIAS
(author of *Can Man Live Without God?* and
Jesus Among Other Gods)

"Joe Boot is a fresh, welcome voice in the Christian world. He presents a clear message that combines intellectual substance and logical development with spiritual enrichment and emotional satisfaction, leaving us not only better informed but under clear urging to respond to the message. He presents the big picture in a way that makes the little things that trouble us fall into place."

—CHARLES PRICE
(Senior Pastor, The People's Church, Toronto, Canada and
former principal of Capernwray Bible School)

"Joe Boot's book is a great read. In a whimsical and thought-provoking way, he builds up his case, chapter after chapter, and draws the reader into the unmistakable weight of the Christian message. His style is wonderfully versatile: narrative, didactive, witty, proclamatory and never dull. Every chapter is a gold mine of stories and insights. And although he signals where he is taking us, there is nothing predictable about Joe's writing. Each argument is alive with a delicious freshness which speaks into the personal lives of his readers, and into the public world today. Joe Boot makes Christianity accessible to anyone who is prepared to read what he says, and I think this could be a key book for years to come."

—DR. ELAINE STORKEY
(broadcaster, international speaker, and member of the
General Synod of the Church of England)

"These pages took my intellect to a place where my heart was ready to cry out to God and he responded."

—ED PILKINGTON
(Website Manager, *Punch* magazine)

"Before exploring this message I had already decided that Christians were deceived in their belief, and that the faith they rejoiced in could offer me nothing; being a barrister I was also ready to argue my corner! But Joe's explanation of Christianity revealed to me the truth and freedom of walking with Jesus Christ as my Lord. God spoke into my heart, both of my desperate need for forgiveness and of God's unfailing love for me nevertheless."
  —ROBERTA PENN
   (barrister)

"Encountering this teaching was like having a blindfold removed—suddenly everything made sense, the way the world is, the way my life is, everything. But even more than the excellent arguments and evidence provided, Joe's obvious love for the truth and for people astounded me and helped me open the door to the greatest love in my life, Jesus."
  —CHARLOTTE HARRIS
   (tax consultant, Arthur Andersen)

"This book will change the way you think, your behavior and your outlook on life. An inspirational read!"
  —STUART HEAD
   (hockey player and Olympian in England)

SEARCHING FOR TRUTH

SEARCHING FOR TRUTH

Discovering the Meaning and Purpose of Life

JOE BOOT

CROSSWAY BOOKS

A DIVISION OF
GOOD NEWS PUBLISHERS
WHEATON, ILLINOIS

Library of Congress Cataloging-in-Publication Data
Boot, Joe, 1974-
    [Time to search]
    Searching for truth : discovering the meaning and purpose of life /
Joe Boot.—1st Crossway ed.
      p. cm.
    Originally published: A time to search. Eastbourne, East Sussex,
England : Kingsway Publications, 2002.
    Includes bibliographical references and index.
    ISBN 1-58134-511-9
    1. Apologetics. I. Title.
BT1103.B66   2003
239—dc21   2003005163

VP		13	12	11	10	09	08	07	06	05	04	03
15	14	13	12	11	10	9	8	7	6	5	4	3	2	1

Dedicated to my brothers,
Jacob (already home), Benjamin, Samuel, and Daniel.
All freed by the Liberator!

contents

Acknowledgments

If good baking is the art of mixing the right ingredients to the correct consistency and timing the cooking length exactly, then writing this book has felt like trying to cook. I trust it is more appetizing than my actual culinary efforts, which my wife tells me leave a lot to be desired! Thankfully I have had help along the way. This book has been in the oven for a number of years, long before I sat at a computer to write. During that time I have been encouraged, inspired, challenged, and shaped by many people to whom I owe a debt of gratitude. I would therefore like to acknowledge a number of people who have played a part in making this book possible and have aided and encouraged me to speak about Jesus Christ in many parts of the world.

Special thanks to my loving parents Michael and Helen, not only for making it easy to obey the fifth commandment, but for being a consistent example of a sacrificial, Christlike life. Thanks to my brothers (to whom this book is dedicated), for your companionship over the years that has proved "a brother is born for adversity." Many thanks to my dear and true friend J. John who believed in me and has invested his very life into my calling ever since. And to my dear friend Charles Price, who by his counsel, teaching, and inspiration has been a constant source of encouragement and spiritual nourishment. Thanks to Andy Economides and Mark Greenwood whose friendship has been utterly dependable and whose thoughtfulness has been a constant challenge to my own thinking. Thanks to my former colleagues and dear friends Jon Paynter, David Robinson, and Judy Moore—you helped shape who I am and what I have written. Thanks to Dave Pope who helped get me going. Thanks to Stuart Lees and

Christ Church Fulham for your encouragement, and for allowing me to forge this material in the rigors of real church life. Special thanks to all my former Vista team and discipleship group whose many comments, reflections, and suggestions illuminated the writing process.

I am indebted to my friends and colleagues Michael Ramsden, Amy Orr-Ewing, and Dr. Elaine Storkey, not only for support and encouragement but for exercising their considerable brainpower in stretching me to think harder and deeper—I could not ask for finer coworkers or better Christian examples. Thank you also to John Earwicker, Moyne Lawson Johnston, and Tim Meathrel for your prayers and encouragement. Special thanks to Dr. Ravi Zacharias for inspirational teaching that has shaped my thinking and for bringing me into his team. Thanks to L.T., my colleague in Singapore whose wisdom has sharpened my mind. Thanks to David Shearman, Gerald Coates, and Malcolm Baxter for their timely words of encouragement and inspiration that have spurred me on. Special thanks to my dear friends Rob and Sandra Lacey whose creativity, radical passion, and insight have touched my heart. Thanks to Zach Watt for your friendship and helpful insights about the manuscript. I would also like to thank Dr. Steve Jones and Dr. Matt Dunkley for their input and expertise on the scientific issues. I enjoyed our many discussions over coffee; your reflections and comments were invaluable.

A special thank you to Richard Herkes, Publishing Director of Kingsway—your enthusiasm for me to write this book, your wit and encouragement, have been much appreciated.

Special thanks to my treasured wife, Jenny. You are my best friend, devoted supporter, finest critic, and loyal partner, who has not only pored over the manuscript for days but has shaped every chapter with keen insight. What would I do without you?

Finally, to him who alone is wise, the immortal, invisible yet personal God, be glory and honor forever and ever. To you I owe all thanks and praise.

Foreword

One of our favorite national pastimes is eating. We do it not only to stay alive but to enjoy ourselves. The biggest selling books are written by chefs, and numerous programs on TV give us new tips to succeed in the kitchen. On both the TV and the printed page the production techniques help make the food look the most exquisite, the most colorful, and the most appetizing. But the problem I have is this: I want to smell it—because actually my hunger for food is brought on by the wonderful aroma. However sophisticated a book is, however wonderful the camera angles are, and however illuminating the lighting in the studio is, it doesn't really do it for me. What I really want are scratch-and-sniff cookbooks, or aroma TV.

That's why this book is brilliant. It's a scratch-and-sniff volume on God. To read this book is to have your senses awakened and set on edge. The aroma creates a desire and longing for God: to see, touch, sense, hear, and taste him. The senses are stimulated as the book throws your eyes to eternity and your ears to the voice that sounds like the rushing of many waters. In its pages Joe Boot leads you to places where you can realize you've been peering through the frosted-up glasses that the world handed you on arrival in the twenty-first century and enables you to see, perhaps for the first time, clearly and to reach out to touch something that in this world of illusion and fantasy is actually solid and real. Joe Boot has done in his first book what many writers haven't managed in ten—he has revealed an appetite for God.

He is like a chef who gets you excited about the food by creating in you a desire for it, an expectation for it, and a longing for the real thing. And this is no reheated meal. Joe skillfully mixes different ingredients together to crack open ancient desires we have had for God from the sixth day of creation. Appealing to head and heart, to imagination and intrigue, to experience and expertise, being thoughtful and thought-provoking, this book fully engages your whole being and makes it impossible to settle for anything less than the real thing.

So I commend Joe Boot to you as a dear friend and one, who in this book, has stimulated in me the most human and God-created desires for intimacy with our God. I encourage you to "taste and see that the Lord is good."

J. John (Founder and President of the Philo Trust)

introduction

The British-American poet T. S. Eliot mused:

> Where is the Life we have lost in living?
> Where is the wisdom we have lost in knowledge?
> Where is the knowledge we have lost in information?
> The cycles of heaven in twenty centuries
> bring us farther from God and nearer to dust.[1]

One of the casualties of our technological age has been the loss of the contemplative life. We assume silence is inimical to living. Now I am not speaking of the demise of monastic life, but specifically of how seldom we devote ourselves to think through life's deep questions and the impact of their answers upon our world. Yes, sometimes such thinking will take place in solitude and silence, but for many, the demands of the moment press upon them to tackle these questions only when deemed necessary or, worse, to detour them altogether. Indeed, as British writer Aldous Huxley once observed, "Most of one's life is one prolonged effort to prevent thinking."

Ironically, however, Huxley's own life was a prolonged restless search for meaning in one relationship and experience after another. He experimented with drugs and various diets, and both he and his wife, Maria, shared an "open" relationship involving other partners while still married. Though he hungered for more, Aldous Huxley admittedly detoured life's deep questions, writing:

> I had motive for not wanting the world to have a meaning; consequently assumed that it had none, and was able without any difficulty to find satisfying reasons for this assumption. The

philosopher who finds no meaning in the world is not concerned exclusively with a problem in pure metaphysics, he is
also concerned to prove that there is no valid reason why he personally should not do as he wants to do, or why his friends
should not seize political power and govern in the way that they
find most advantageous to themselves. . . . For myself, the philosophy of meaninglessness was essentially an instrument of
liberation, sexual and political.[2]

Nonetheless, the price paid for such a conflicted life is devastating. As Jesus reminds us, "For where your treasure is, there your heart
will be also."[3] In fact, the Scriptures place supreme value on one's
thought life. "For as he thinketh in his heart, so is he," King Solomon
wrote of man.[4] Of course, Solomon knew about this restless search for
meaning: "I denied myself nothing my eyes desired; I refused my heart
no pleasure. . . . Yet when I surveyed all that my hands had done and
what I had toiled to achieve, everything was meaningless, a chasing
after the wind."[5] Ultimately, Solomon concluded that life apart from
God is meaningless and repeated his injunction to all who will listen:
"Remember your Creator."[6]

Remember. Consider. Think. If we long for our lives to flourish, we
must pause first to consider the deep questions of life, for in truth they
are inescapable. Hence I am delighted to recommend this book by my
colleague Joe Boot, for who is more fitting to guide us through these
questions than a young man with a passion and vision for our world
rooted in his knowledge and love for God.

In his devotional *Filled with the Spirit*, Richard Ellsworth Day
makes this perceptive observation:

It would be no surprise, if a study of secret causes were undertaken, to find that every golden era in human history proceeds
from the devotion and righteous passion of some single individual. This does not set aside the sovereignty of God; it simply
indicates the instrument through which He uniformly works.
There are no bona fide mass movements; it just looks that way.
At the center of the column there is always one [person] who
knows his God, and knows where he is going.[7]

There is a weight of truth in that statement. And every now and then our lives cross the path of one in whose life you sense a uniqueness and anointing. Joe Boot is such a man. I have known Joe and his lovely wife, Jenny, for some time now. They are a blessing to know, and it is a privilege to work alongside them. Joe's authenticity and calling shine through this work. He is young in years but mature in insight. He is gentle in spirit but intense in conviction. He is eager to speak but careful to listen. He helps find answers because he understands the search.

This book reveals those marvelous combinations. Joe addresses the deepest quest of the human heart—to make sense out of life's most probing questions and to sensibly give answers. His book covers a wide range of issues, but at its core it connects with the individual reader to disclose our heart's real search and God's soul-touching response. In *Searching for Truth* you will find a place to find answers. After all, God says in His Word, "You shall search for me and find me when you shall search for me with all your heart."[8]

Ravi Zacharias

preface

King Solomon wrote, "Of making many books there is no end."[1] So why should I be seeking to add more weight to your shelves? I hope only to inspire you to take down (or buy a copy of) one of the oldest volumes in the world—the Bible—then to blow the dust from the cover and search for the meaning of life through the unique Person revealed in its pages. A. W. Tozer once suggested that the only books that should really be written are those that force themselves out from you of necessity. I am glad to say that this has been the case for me with this labor of love.

This book began life as a series of talks about Christianity given while I was working as an evangelist in southwest London. The talks were formed into a six-week course called Vista, which was attended by various skeptical people through several terms. Some of the comments of a few of those people are found at the beginning of this book. I discovered that many people have ignored or rejected Christianity, not because they have investigated it, understood it, and found it wanting, but because they had not addressed or answered the many questions they had about it credibly. Or in other cases they had never had Christianity or the Bible explained to them in a way that made any sense. I also noted that increasing numbers of people have practically no knowledge of the Bible at all. Consequently many Christian communicators are answering questions people are not asking and are also using language and terms incomprehensible to the majority of people when left unexplained. Given that many people's understanding of Christianity is now a misunderstanding, I felt compelled to write this book and was strongly urged to do so by many who attended the course.

I have therefore written primarily for people searching for answers in their lives to those vague yet persistent longings for God, for forgiveness, for meaning, and for purpose, and for those seeking a reasonable explanation of the Christian faith that makes sense of our twenty-first-century world. Jean-Paul Sartre, the famed atheist, once confessed:

> As for me, I don't see myself as so much dust that has appeared in the world but as a being that was expected, prefigured, called forth. In short, as a being that could, it seems, come only from a creator; and this idea of a creating hand that created me refers me back to God. Naturally this is not a clear, exact idea that I set in motion every time I think of myself. It contradicts many of my other ideas; but it is there, floating vaguely. And when I think of myself I often think rather in this way, for want of being able to think otherwise.[2]

We all have these convictions either buried deep or on the surface, expressed or left unarticulated. So this is where we begin, with our vague assumptions, and then we move from our own human convictions about life to the worldview of the Bible and the life of Jesus Christ and his claims. Along the way we will wrestle with many questions about suffering, truth, morality, and guilt. My hope is that you will enjoy the journey and at the very least be inspired to search for truth wherever it is found.

I must confess that there is nothing truly new in this book—at least I certainly hope not! I would have failed in my purpose if there is. The role of the Christian apologist is not to reinvent Christianity; it would cease to be Christianity if he or she did! The Bible is not a book we are to update, but one we should seek to understand and test for truth. The role of the Christian apologist in a changing world is to explain the Bible's unchanging message for his or her generation in a way that can be understood, offering logical reasons for its validity. The questions "is it true?" and "does it work?" are paramount as we search out the meaning of life.

If you are extremely skeptical about Christianity for whatever reason, you may already be tempted to put this book down and do something else. I have not sought to hide that this book explores Christianity, as I have no desire to deceive any reader. But I would simply challenge you to read on and have the courage to face yourself and your position. Searching for truth and examining the questions of life will not do any of us any harm, only good. We have nothing to fear from thinking! Let us seek to think as clearly as we can.

Pascal wrote:

> Many people hate religion. And hatred is deepened because they are afraid it might be true. The cure for this is first to show that religion is not contrary to reason, and thus should be taken seriously. Secondly, make religion attractive, so that good people want it to be true. Thirdly, explain to them that religion can help them to understand themselves, and in this way bring them many blessings.[3]

That appropriately summarizes the aim of this book. The wise King Solomon tells us there is "a time to search,"[4] and my sincere desire is that you will read this book and discover that life is far more wonderful, and its possibilities, purpose and joys more amazing, than you had previously ever imagined.

Joe Boot

1

LOOK AT THAT VIEW!

To get the best out of life, great matters have to be given a second thought.

BLAISE PASCAL

A VIEW TO A LIFE

It is often said that a spectacular view makes you feel closer to God; perhaps it is the magnificence, the clarity of vision it affords. For me, there are few things more satisfying than arduous walking; a good hike can be laborious but more often than not, the harder the ascent, the more amazing the view.

Hay Stacks in the Lake District is one of my favorite climbs. Initially the going is easy; then all of a sudden you are confronted with a steep ascent between two crags that can take a couple of hours. You have to grit your teeth and go for it, pausing for breath and drinking plenty of water on the way up. During these interludes you can turn and look at where you have come from to gain encouragement. But standing on the summit—that's the moment! The wind is strong, gusting round about you, the heart is racing, and your legs are tired, but you feel as though you are standing on the roof of the world. The birds are flying beneath you, and nothing can be heard but the wind and falling water. Lifting your eyes, you can see for miles (weather permitting!) across land and lake. In those moments I wish I had wings, as the thought of flight is hard to resist. Taking in this perfect vista makes all the pain worthwhile. It's no surprise that from such a vantage point you see the landscape as you have never seen it before.

A vista is a view. How we view things affects our perception of the world in which we live. How we view things helps shape our understanding of reality itself. Dense tropical vegetation and tall trees, for example, surround tribal people living in the Amazon; so they never see large open spaces. Their spatial awareness is limited to their environment; to them the world is a thicket. If they are taken to large open areas, travel in an aircraft, or look at the sea, their brains take time to adjust and learn how to judge distance and understand perspective. In fact, every human brain has to learn perspective.

This principle is true not just of our physical eyesight but of our human understanding; it is true of our minds. A vista can also be a mental vision. Our mental view is the way in which we reason about the world, life and living, death and dying. In short it is our worldview. It is possible and even common for us to give this matter so little thought that we are in fact like the tribesmen—unable to see the wood for the trees, without a true perspective and unable to reach a vantage point from which to view reality. Until we stop, hold back the incessant rush of our lives, and consider our worldview, we remain caught in a mental thicket, unaware of the nature of our situation.

Each of us has a worldview whether we realize it or not. All of us operate from some framework or another, however simple or ill thought out it may be. The assumptions we have about the makeup of our world constitute our worldview. It is this framework that allows us to think at all! Our ability to think and to reason about our lives and our universe is one of the things that separates us from the animal kingdom. We are capable of connected thought; we are able to consider complex alternatives and come to conclusions.

Almost Unbelievable

I recently read a remarkable little story about people living in the town of Fyffe in the American state of Alabama. Some residents made the extraordinary claim that in February 1989 the recently departed pianist

Liberace treated them to a concert from beyond the grave. Apparently he descended from a golden banana-shaped spacecraft. The twelve-foot-tall "ivory tinkler" was then brought to earth by a magical escalator, where he thrilled the crowds with songs from his shows, playing a floating piano. The rumor of this remarkable "comeback gig" spread quickly throughout the area, causing a sensation. Eventually the police were called in to clear a traffic jam of an estimated four thousand cars that had built up along the roads into the town center.

I shall leave you to draw your own conclusions about this report; we are able as human beings to weigh it all. We almost unconsciously test its validity as our minds examine it in the light of our worldview. Most of us would smile, allow ourselves a little chuckle, and file it under fiction! Nonetheless it is incredible what some of us will swallow without consideration or thought.

It is no less remarkable what many of us will reject with equally little thought and total disregard for the evidence. Apparently there remains an organization today called the Flat-Earth Society. They believe that the earth is flat and that pictures taken from orbit revealing the earth as a sphere are high-level government hoaxes. When we humans gather in numbers, it does seem that we have a tendency not to think for ourselves but instead to follow the crowd, even in stupidity. In 1878 a British Parliamentary Committee was set up to review Thomas Edison's invention of the light bulb. They duly concluded, "It is good enough for our transatlantic friends but unworthy of the attention of practical or scientific men."[1]

Prejudice, pride, laziness, fear, and stubbornness all play a part in the adopting of such an unthinking attitude. We know this is true in our everyday lives. Most of the trifling conflict that I have with my wife arises when one of us (usually me) is too stubborn or proud to admit that he or she is wrong. When Christopher Columbus set out to prove that the earth is round, many rejected the idea as ludicrous, despite a wealth of evidence that he was right. When Galileo sought to show that the earth was in motion and not static, he was considered insane because his opponents had such unbending ideas about the universe. Their worldview was based on inaccurate Greek metaphysics, and their minds were made up, so Galileo had to be wrong!

They were more committed to a system of thought than to discovering the truth. Unless we wish to plead insanity, we must accept that "the truth is out there," and if we have integrity we shall want to embrace that truth. Truth matters; so the matter of truth deserves our thought and attention.

JUST THINKING

Not to think with careful consideration about our lives and the world in which we live can be a foolish mistake. Indeed, it can be far worse than being pigheaded about some point of science. The reason is clear. The ramifications of what we think are far-reaching! How we view life is ultimately that which gives to us meaning, value, and purpose. These primary principles in turn dramatically affect our behavior. In other words, what we believe determines how we behave. The importance of this is obvious. People who, in a twisted state of mind, believe that certain immoral acts are more meaningful than goodness or self-control invariably commit atrocities like murder, rape, child abuse, and terrorism. Such acts demonstrate a state of mind that values selfishness more than any other consideration, and we are rightly afraid of those who have such an attitude and belief.

What we believe to be true always invests our lives with meaning of some sort, even if we believe life is purposeless and has no ultimate meaning. Because any truth claim must be meaningful, this philosophy of meaninglessness gives us a contradiction: The meaning of life is that it has no meaning. This is not sound reasoning.

It is unavoidable that belief determines behavior; it is a law of our minds. If in a final warning our boss tells us we shall be fired if we are late for work once more, and we like our job, we would consider the threat meaningful and arrive on time. If we believe our bus timetable, we shall follow its instructions. Although it sometimes feels like it, nobody waits for a bus not scheduled to come!

THE REALLY BIG ISSUE

So what is it that we really believe to be true? Think for a moment about some of the big questions of life.

- Who are we?
- Where did we come from?
- What does it mean to be human?
- What is truth?
- What is the meaning and purpose of life?
- Why is there so much evil in the world?
- How should we live?
- What happens when we die?
- Does it matter?

Our worldview determines how we seek to solve these problems. Ask yourself how you view life. How often do you think about it? Before moving on in this book, think for a few moments about some of these questions.

Often time to think about such things only comes when our head hits the pillow, and it's not long before our thoughts become convoluted and we drift off to sleep. The radio wakes us again in the morning with the traffic report, the news, the weather, and the incessant babble of the breakfast DJ. "Real life" hits us smack in the face. People to see, places to go, trains to catch, e-mails to send, money to make, children to bring up—the list is endless. Time to think in the twenty-first century is in short supply. The pace of life for the most part is fast and furious, but somehow we need to set aside time.

WHAT ON EARTH!

Thinking is fine, but what on earth are we supposed to examine? Is there anything worth serious consideration? Our world is a deeply confusing and trying place sending us mixed messages. A friend recently said to me that he "just didn't know what to believe anymore." Fewer people have firm convictions about anything—even politics! As a society we are disillusioned with authority, politicians, policemen, priests, and presidents. We are tired of empty words and broken promises; the hypocrisy simply wears us out. Why is it that in a culture so technologically advanced and more educated than ever, so many people are tired, lost, and hopelessly adrift? Many of us willingly confess that though pleasures and plenty surround our lives, we feel spiritually empty.

A seemingly endless stream of public figures, pop stars, million-aires, and Hollywood celebrities end up exposing their own despair in a glossy centerfold. Others, in even more tragic circumstances, seek escape from life altogether. Kurt Cobain and Michael Hutchence are just two contemporary megastars who have taken their own lives. Life, it seems, has never been more uncertain. So many of us do not know what to believe anymore, and hence we do not know how to live, which leaves us in a mess.

We are now all too familiar with rising crime figures; watching Crimewatch UK [in England or similar programs in the U.S.] is usu-ally a horrifying ordeal. Juvenile delinquency has rocketed out of all proportion, with a considerable percentage of violent crime now being committed by those as young as ten. This is a society my grandpar-ents would not recognize; so the unsuspecting elderly are often on the receiving end of its horrors. I need not go on to discuss police cor-ruption, the near-impossible task of many schoolteachers, assaults on doctors, child abuse, sports hooligans, political sleaze, calculated medical malpractice, and genocide on three continents including Europe—and now we are faced with mass terrorism. This sort of bad news is practically the norm. It takes a lot to shock a twenty-first-cen-tury individual. Our familiarity with unthinkable evil means that much of it leaves us feeling numb. But we each have a duty to ask, "What is wrong with the world? Where is it all going? How should I respond to this?"

WAKE-UP CALL

The philosopher Socrates said, "The unexamined life is not worth liv-ing."[2] Surely he was right. It is only when we examine our lives that we truly come to understand ourselves or what it is to be human. By this process we grow up. The longer we put it off, the longer we play in the nursery of our ignorance.

It is essential for each of us to consider our ways regardless of our age, education, or position. The book you are holding in your hand is an opportunity for you to do just that. It is our ways that we need to consider—the way we think and the way we live. It is time to stop and examine our worldview with its implications for life and living, death and dying. The time is right for us to get things in their true perspective. To some extent we have all allowed television, videos, magazines, and websites to do too much of our thinking for us. The dietitians tell us that we are what we eat; it is equally true that we are what we read. Or to be more precise, what we feed our minds (whatever the medium) is what we become. Serious reading is growing less popular today because our culture has become highly visual. Some statisticians reckon that the majority of homes in Britain now have no books at all!

Because television soaps, films, computer games, the Net, and the pop industry dominate our recreational lives, it does seem we are becoming shallower. Many cultural analysts agree that in many ways we are amusing ourselves to death. We tend to ignore, or at least rarely think deeply about, the big picture of life, because we have little time for the labor of thinking when there is so much to entertain. These things are rarely wrong in themselves, but it is their domination in our lives that affects our ability to think clearly for ourselves and therefore becomes destructive. This book is not an appeal to open new libraries or crack down on the Net! Neither is it only intended for people with an academic or intellectual leaning. In fact, it is my hope that people who have never seriously considered their worldview will read this profitably. It does not concern mere abstract concepts but the very heart of our everyday lives.

The simple challenge of this book is to consider your ways. One of the most irritating questions that children repeatedly ask is "Why?" Annoying it can be, but essential it is! That question enables them to learn, mature, and grow. Sadly, as we enter adulthood we ask "Why?" fewer and fewer times, never mind seek to answer it! Perhaps it is for fear of what the answer may be.

For a moment now, with childlike boldness, face yourself. Consider your very existence; consider your life. What do you believe? Why do you believe it? How does it impact your life?

These are sobering thoughts. Yet these are undoubtedly the most important questions we can ever ask. It is our ability to think and ask such questions that sets us apart.

Blaise Pascal wrote:

Humanity is only a reed, the weakest reed in nature. But humanity is a thinking reed. The universe does not make any effort to crush humanity; human beings are easily killed. But even if the rest of the universe were to turn against humanity, humanity alone would understand what was happening—because humanity alone possesses the power of thought. All our dignity consists in this power. Our survival depends on this power. Our knowledge of morality, and thence how we should behave, depends on this power. So let us strive to think well.[3]

COME, LET US REASON!

It may be a surprise to many that one book that constantly calls us to consider our ways and think well about our lives is the Bible. In fact, far from being an antiquated or irrelevant book of rules, the Bible presents a compelling perspective on reality that, if accurate, is a vista with far-reaching implications for us all. I share the belief of many millions today and throughout history that there is no view of the universe that speaks more accurately about what is or has a greater ring of truth about it than the worldview of the Bible. No message I have ever heard speaks with greater relevance about life itself than the one found in this remarkable book.

Far from the mythical image of an aloof and disinterested God thundering down arbitrary rules from on high, the Bible presents a personal God who calls us to "reason" with him concerning our lives. The commands for living that he gives are neither arbitrary nor repressive, but sound instruction in accord with what we know in our own consciences to be right. In the Bible, God is revealed as One who speaks and acts for the good of the universe and all his creatures. The central figure of the Bible on which all else depends is the persistent, unique, and powerful person of Jesus Christ. Remarkably he claimed that he himself was the embodiment of truth. He declared that his teaching about the world and the needs of us all as people revealed the only true way to understand life itself.

The new life that Jesus Christ calls all people to in Scripture has become known as Christianity. It is the worldview and message of Christianity that is the primary subject of this book, and for good reason: Given the nature of Christ's claims and actions, we shall see that the Christian message stands unique among all other messages. It has been both greatly loved and greatly opposed, yet it remains the most enduring motivation for change, future hope, life, and purpose that the world has ever known. Rooted in history and proven relevant for two millennia, biblical Christianity stands as the message of all messages to be reckoned with in the twenty-first century. So by investigating this, we shall be invited to consider our ways.

Given the unique claims of Jesus Christ and the Bible, it is imperative that we examine them carefully and reach a conclusion. It is impossible to be neutral about Jesus Christ! Concerning the Christian faith C. S. Lewis wrote, "If it is false, it is of no importance; if true, it is of infinite importance. The one thing it cannot be is moderately important."[4]

Lewis put it like this in order to emphasize that the message of Christ is unique and that we have to decide what we believe about it, because if it is true, it must be acted upon. Matthew Parris (*The Times* columnist) seems to have understood this implication when he wrote:

> If I believed that [what Christians say about the possibility of knowing God] or even a tenth of that . . . I would drop my job, sell my house, throw away my possessions, leave my acquaintances and set out into the world with a burning desire to know more and, when I had found out more, to act upon it and tell others. . . . I am unable to understand how anyone who believed what is written in the Bible could choose to spend his waking hours in any other endeavour.[5]

While the Bible does not tell everybody to do the things Mr. Parris says he would do if he considered Christianity true, his point is a vital one. For as we have seen, belief affects behavior; and if the message of Christ is right and not wrong, if it is true and not false, it is of the greatest possible significance to us all.

For a variety of reasons most people's understanding of Christianity is a misunderstanding. Popular myths include the idea that it consists of a code of ethics, the repression of sex, generally being kind, going to church on Sundays, being born in a Christian country, believing disproved nonsense, living in the irrelevant past, and generally being an ignorant bore. Now before we accept or reject something that is presented to us, it is vital that we understand it first. If we reject a Christianity of our own imagining, we have simply knocked down a straw man. It is my intention to bring before you, to the best of my ability, the real message for you to consider. To get through and enjoy this book you will only need an open mind to "come and reason" and a genuine desire to check it out thoroughly for yourself.

MESSAGE IN A BOTTLE: THE STORY OF JACK WURM

Walking one day along the California coast, Jack was musing about his life. His marriage was in trouble, he was not getting on well with his kids, and he was unsure of what he was doing with his future. As he strolled along, a shiny object glinted in the sunshine and caught his eye. Going over for a closer look, he discovered an old bottle washed up on the shore. Picking it up, he noticed that the cap was still on, and there appeared to be a note inside. His curiosity was aroused; so he smashed the bottle on a large pebble and took out the note to examine it. It read, "I Daisy Alexander do hereby will my entire estate to the lucky person who finds this note and to my attorney Mr B Cowin. June 30, 1936." Obviously his first thought was that it was the work of a creative prankster. He was about to throw the note away; but caught in two minds, he folded it up and put it in his pocket.

Not long after this incident he bumped into a friend of his who happened to be a lawyer. Jack told him about the message in the bottle and asked him what he thought. The attorney told Jack he should investigate it. Jack protested that the idea was stupid, that he would only be made to look like a fool investigating such a ridiculous note. However, his friend encouraged him to find out whether or not it was true. "You will be a bigger fool if you don't check it out," he told him.

To make a long story short, Jack Wurm did investigate the note. The process took him to the highest courts in the United States. The evidence showed conclusively that Daisy Alexander had existed, that her home had been in London, and that she was the heiress to the Singer sewing machine fortune. She had left a separate will, and in it she stated that whoever found the piece of paper could have half her money. (It turned out that she was a highly eccentric lady!) One morning she had written the note, placed it in the bottle, and thrown it into the River Thames. One of the experts called to give evidence was a mathematician. He calculated that a bottle thrown into the Thames would do the following: From the Thames it would enter the North Sea, then flow eventually into the Bering Sea and on into the Pacific. He worked out that in the unlikely event of a bottle surviving such an incredible journey, it would take twelve years for the bottle to get from the Thames to California. It actually took eleven and a half years! Jack Wurm inherited three and a half million dollars!

This incredible story of Jack Wurm and the will in a bottle would never have been told if he had thrown away the message. All that inheritance would have been lost. If his friend had not cajoled him into investigating the message to test its truth, Jack would have remained a relatively poor man. Instead, because he examined the whole matter, what had at first appeared foolish proved to be a remarkable reality! Even a message that at first seems hard to believe or understand can bring a great reward.

LADIES AND GENTLEMEN OF THE JURY . . .

The Christian message revealed in the Bible is of far greater significance than Jack's message in a bottle and promises much more than money. Investigating and examining it is potentially far more rewarding. In the story we have just read, a careful examination of the message was followed by an assessment of the evidence. The truth was determined, and the reward followed. Exactly the same thing is required with Christianity. We must look at the message, examine the evidence, hear the witnesses, and reach a verdict.

In the United Kingdom [and in the U.S. as well] we have a judicial system that allows us to be tried by a jury of our peers. Any of us at any time may be called upon to take up jury service. As you read this book it may help you to put yourself in the position of a juror, summoned to hear a critical case. You are intimately involved with all the proceedings; you are not merely observing the case as a spectator. Consider yourself as one hearing a case about which you will have to deliver a verdict. The media has published all sorts of things about the case that are inaccurate and misinformed; unavoidably, to some degree, these things may have biased your thinking. However, you are being asked by the court not to allow this to cloud your judgment as you hear the evidence. You must consider it all carefully. It is important that you use your intuition as much as your reasoning powers as you look at the issues, engaging your heart as well as your head. Listen to the facts, follow the arguments, test the character of the witnesses, be guided by your conscience, and consider your verdict.

Now if all that sounds like too much hard work, I offer this thought that has always helped me: Raking is easy, and digging is hard. But with a rake all you get is leaves; with a spade you may find gold or buried treasure.

2

Beyond Reasonable Doubt

More consequences for thought and action follow from the affirmation or denial of God than from answering any other question.

MORTIMER ADLER, COEDITOR,
ENCYCLOPAEDIA BRITANNICA

GOD IN THE SHED

Ben was only eight and afraid of the dark. One evening his mother was cleaning the kitchen and wanted to sweep out the hall; so she asked him to fetch her the broom from the shed. Startled by such a suggestion Ben turned to her and said, "But, Mum, I don't want to go out there; it's really dark." His mother looked at him with a reassuring smile and said, "Now you know you don't need to be afraid of the dark, Ben. God is out there. He will protect you; so go on, and sing on the way." Looking quizzically at his mother, Ben sought further confirmation. "Are you sure he's out there?" "Yes, of course I'm sure. God is everywhere, and he is always ready to help if you need him," answered his mother confidently. Ben thought about this for a few moments and then walked cautiously toward the back door. Slowly he opened it halfway and peered through the gap. Then, raising his voice, he called out, "God? If you are out there, would you please fetch me the broom from the shed?"

In order to begin we must start at the beginning! The most fundamental of all questions that can possibly be asked is, "Does God exist?" That is not to say that it is the foremost question on everybody's mind. You may well have decided that there is a God and have other questions that are far more important to you than this one: How can I find peace and happiness? What does the future hold? How can I solve my personal problems? Other questions of this sort may be far more prominent issues to you. However, the existence of God has huge implications for all these others. It is with this ultimate question that our hearing must begin. Either God exists or he does not. There is no middle ground. Both cannot be true. No amount of philosophical trickery can hide from the greatest antithesis of them all. Either God is or he is not. We cannot leave this question for the intellectuals, scientists, philosophers, and theologians alone; we must answer it as well. We must answer it for ourselves.

Believing in God, however, is not like other things we can "believe" in:

> The Loch Ness Monster is merely "one more thing." . . . God, however, is not merely "one more thing." The person who believes in God and the person who does not believe in God do not merely disagree about God. They disagree about the very character of the universe.[1]

Everything that can be said about human life and behavior comes all the way back to this. Our convictions on this point unavoidably determine what we can or cannot legitimately believe concerning all other fundamental questions.

POLL POSITION!

Many surveys have been conducted worldwide on the subject of religious belief. These statistics are at the best of times ambiguous because any question about God needs qualifying. For example, some people believe in a personal God of creation, whereas others believe God to be a "life force"—impersonal and unknowable. Some scientists have even smuggled into a materialist worldview a god of cosmic dust, mysteriously interwoven with the fabric of the universe. So a definition of what we mean by *God* is crucial. We shall consider this later.

However, universal belief in a Supreme Being is still as persistent as ever. A worldwide poll taken in 1991 has the global figure for atheists at just 4.4 percent.[2] Another category titled "other non-religious" added a further 16.4 percent—agnostics in the "don't know" camp probably account for most of these. That leaves nearly 80 percent of the world's population professing belief in some sort of God.

In the United Kingdom at the end of 1999 a British survey conducted by Opinion Research Business suggested that 38 percent were "not religious."[3] This figure would again include both atheists and agnostics.

HUMAN INTUITION

What do these figures tell us? Perhaps many reasonable deductions could be made, but the obvious one is this: Most people instinctively or intuitively believe in God. If the poll had included a question on one's familiarity with the major arguments for the existence of God, I suspect 99 percent would have denied any such specialized knowledge. So belief in God goes well beyond reason and argument; it seems to reside in our very nature. The atheist often finds that he is at odds with himself and the world around him. He must continually search for reasons to reject the existence of God. He must deny his own intuition and try to rationalize the notion that the universe has sprung into being without cause, without mind, and without design.

On the other hand, people who believe in God rarely find themselves wrestling with their intellects, desperately trying to find some shred of evidence that may point to the reality of a "Supreme Being." Their heart tells them he is. Conscience shouts it, and reason seems to demand it. Of course, big questions still remain, but the essential conviction that he is real is common and hard to dispute.

CHILD PRODIGY

This intuitive belief is found in children all over the world. I was sent an e-mail about an eight-year-old boy from Chula Vista, California, who was given a stretching homework assignment, a challenge beyond the reach of the greatest minds. He was asked to explain God! This is what he wrote:

> One of God's main jobs is making people. He makes them to replace the ones that die, so there will be enough people to take care of things on earth. He doesn't make grown ups, just babies. I think because they are smaller and easier to make. That way he doesn't have to take up his valuable time teaching them to talk and walk, he can just leave that to mothers and fathers. God's second most important job is listening to prayers. An awful lot of this goes on, since some people, like preachers and things, pray at times besides bedtime. God doesn't have time to listen to the radio or T.V. because of this. Because he hears everything, there must be a terrible lot of noise in his ears, unless he has thought of a way to turn it off. . . . God sees everything and hears everything and is everywhere, which keeps him pretty busy. So you shouldn't go wasting his time by going over your mom and dad's head asking for things they said you couldn't have. . . . If you don't believe in God you will be very lonely, because your parents can't go everywhere with you like to camp, but God can. It is good to know he's around you when you're scared in the dark or when you can't swim and you get thrown into real deep water by big kids. But you shouldn't just always think of what God can do for you.
>
> I figure God put me here and he can take me back anytime he pleases. And that's why I believe in God.[4]

Anthropologists have discovered this sort of thinking in children everywhere, even in places where the religious culture teaches something different.

THE BURDEN OF PROOF

Now obviously just because the vast majority of people believe in God or a god of some kind, we cannot conclusively say, "God exists." Universal belief in God throughout known history is a significant argument, but it doesn't amount to proof.

There is a huge problem with the issue of proof. Due to our limited minds, the nature of the issue we are dealing with puts proof practically out of the question. Some philosophers believe that even to attempt to prove the issue is futile. It is fair to say that the question of the existence of God can be neither philosophically proved nor disproved by human reason alone. By that I do not mean that we cannot be convinced about God's existence. We certainly can be. I simply mean that the existence of God cannot be demonstrated so as to convince everybody.

The media, as well as our own schooling, can give us the impression that science and scientific laws are provable, whereas God, the Bible, or Christianity are not. This is a misconception (though a forgivable one)! To do justice to our discussion we must take a brief look at this issue. If you don't want a gentle mental workout and have no interest in the nature of proof, you may wish to skip the next few pages, but do not miss out on what is being said here!

FULL PROOF?

Logic demands that only deductive knowledge is strictly provable. To deduce something we must start with a truth definitely known and then by the logical process of inference arrive at certain facts that bring us to a conclusion. But what do we definitely know in order to begin this process? You may have heard the philosopher René Descartes's famous inductive argument about his own existence: "I think; therefore I am." He believed this was all he could be certain of as a basis for deductive reasoning. Though not exact logic (i.e., who is "I"?), we know what he was getting at. Others have even doubted that! However, insanity is not our current inquiry, so let me get to the point. Some philosophers and thinkers believe there is no a priori knowledge, no innate, intuitive truth. In other words, they believe that nothing is simply known. Many others dispute that, as I do, but it highlights an important point. Much of what we believe to be certain knowledge is not deductive at all. This is particularly important when considering the claims of some scientists and the popular belief that science only deals in certain knowledge.

The essence of the scientific method is what is called empiricism (the acquisition of knowledge through the experiences of our senses).

Science, then, does not begin with what is definitely known. Instead, it allows evidence, which must be interpreted, to lead the inquirer where it will. Our scientific laws are simply the result of observed uniformities. If I let go of my car keys, they fall to the ground. This happens each time I drop them; so we theorize and construct the Law of Gravity. Although we accept this as a fact, it is not proved as such. Instead, we have reached a conclusion (or proposed a theory) by induction, not deduction. Induction is a philosophical term given to the process of using evidence to reach a wider conclusion: The evidence infers that your conclusion is the best explanation.

Sherlock Holmes is often thought of as the detective who solves his case by brilliant deduction (where the conclusion logically follows the premise). However, this is not entirely accurate. Despite the claims of his creator, Sir Arthur Conan Doyle, Holmes's methods are nearly always inductive. In the story *A Study in Scarlet*, Holmes describes the secret of his own work:

> Like all other arts the science of deduction and analysis is one which can only be acquired by long and patient study. . . . On meeting a fellow mortal, learn at a glance to distinguish the history of the man, and the trade or profession to which he belongs. . . . By a man's finger nails, by his coat sleeve, by his boots, by his trouser knees, by the callosities of his forefinger and thumb, by his expression, by his shirt cuffs—by each of these things a man's calling is plainly revealed.[5]

It is by careful observation that Sherlock Holmes gathers evidence to reach a wider conclusion about a certain character to solve his case. And this is induction, not deduction! In truth, this is the process by which both science and history operate. Neither can be "proved" in the deductive sense. Scientific and historical propositions are accepted or rejected depending on how convincing the evidence is and whether independent testimonies are competent and reliable.

A lot of our human knowledge is acquired through the process of induction. Think how children learn. Simply telling a child not to touch the fire or not to stand up on the chair is often not enough; they have to find out for themselves! They soon learn that fire is hot and burns when you touch it and that the ground is hard and hurts when you fall on it from a height. When we are young, our time is spent finding out about the world we live in; in fact, this process never stops. Largely unconsciously, we gather millions of bits of information and become certain about many things we now take for granted. For example: rain is wet and cool. This becomes a certain premise. We then make deductions based on that reasonable fact. For example: rain is not hot and dry. If you stand in the rain, you will get wet. If you leave your washing on the line when it rains, it will get soaked. These deductions are logically valid as they are deduced from what, for all practical purposes, is a known fact—they are deduced from a known quantity. So, provided my initial exercise in induction is correct, my deductions are valid.

Now obviously we cannot show that there is a known quantity greater or further back than God from which he can be deduced—the very idea is a contradiction because God is the name we give to an ultimate being who is logically required. He is therefore the necessary cause and source of all things. So proving the existence of God deductively is impossible. Equally, proving God does not exist is impossible. Science, which seeks to define and categorize our reality, as we have seen, is not provable. In science there is no certainty, only high or low probability. Any scientific hypothesis only requires one contrary instance to pull the whole thing down. For several hundred years Newton's theories seemed to be proven, and then along came Einstein. Who knows what will be next? Molecular biologist Dr. Andrew Miller says, "It is certainly not a scientific matter to decide whether or not there is a God."[6]

All our knowledge, then, is an intricate combination of intuition (first truths), induction, and deduction. Philosophers will always argue about which comes first and how much we can truly know. I believe the truth can be discovered in each of these ways and that it is foolish to exclude any of them. In reality, the way we arrive at the truth is not complicated at all. We deduce things from what we innately know (a priori), and the experience of being alive in this world gives us compelling evidence to reach, by inference (induction), reliable conclusions.

I am in no doubt: I feel as certain of the existence of God as I am about my own existence. God is a logically required being; I am not! However, my confidence is not based on a scientific experiment in a laboratory or on a brilliantly reasoned argument from a philosopher. My convictions are the result of the above combination of factors. Reason (inductive and deductive), faith, experience, revelation, history, conscience, and intuition all play a part. As human beings we are more than pure reason. Mind is more than merely intellect. Life is more than an equation. For example: I am in love with my wife. I know this to be true. I am as certain of this as I am of the fact that I was born in London and grew up in the West Country. I can't prove that to you. I cannot give you an equation for love. I would be a wealthy man if I could. I cannot conclusively demonstrate this love with a scientific experiment, but it is no less true. Blaise Pascal hit the nail on the head when he said, "The heart has its reasons of which reason knows nothing."[7] In the same way, while conclusive philosophic "proof" may be forever out of reach, being convinced of God's existence is not.

BEYOND REASON

One of the most important things that reason and intelligence can do for us is make us aware of our own limitations. Some of the greatest thinkers in the history of the world have endeavored to point this out.

In 1932 Albert Einstein wrote in a letter to Queen Elizabeth of Belgium, "As a human being one has been endowed with intelligence to be able to see clearly how utterly inadequate that intelligence is when confronted with what exists."[8] We should avoid at all costs an arrogance that believes human intellect alone can plumb the depths of the mysteries around us. The advice of Einstein must surely be applied to this great consideration of the being of God. We cannot reject the existence of his being simply because we are unable to comprehend him fully. That would be like throwing away a priceless book simply because it was written in a language we have not yet learned.

No human being will ever master God, for he cannot be reduced to an equation on a chalkboard, handled and classified by a scientist or philosopher. If that were possible we would be the gods. If God is real, then he is the giver of mind, thought, and intellect. Our very ability to reason comes from him. The created, and consequently finite, minds of people are incapable of fully comprehending the infinite and self-existent. As Pascal wrote, "Reason's last step is the recognition that there are an infinite number of things which are beyond it. It is merely feeble if it does not go as far as to realise that."[9] The cosmos is full of great wonders. The more marvels we uncover, the more awestruck and perplexed we are. The more of nature's shoreline we find, the greater the vast waves of the unknown that break upon us. We are like children playing in the rock pools of knowledge, while as far as the eye can see an incalculable ocean of mystery thunders, roars, and overwhelms.

As we explore a fraction of our amazing universe, we come face to face with a profound truth: Someone infinitely more marvelous than we can possibly imagine is the architect of our reality. So while we admit we cannot have deductive proof of God's existence, we have evidence that amounts to an overwhelmingly compelling case—we can achieve a balance of probability that goes way beyond reasonable doubt.

KNOCK, KNOCK!

Who is out there? Who is God? Before we look at a few simple reasons why God is both real and relevant, we must define our terms. What do we mean by *God*? About whom are we talking? When I was studying philosophy of religion and moral ethics at college, our teacher came up with a name for God in which each letter represented one or more of his characteristics. It was an extremely helpful way of remembering who we were talking about when we referred to God. We reverently called him PHILCOG.

P Personal

God is not a thing, energy, or force. He thinks, he feels, he acts; he is a person.

H Holy

God is morally perfect. He has no failing or deficiency. He is utterly flawless in his being and his actions.

I Infinite, Immanent, Immutable

(a) God is self-existent. Nobody created him. He had no beginning and will have no end. He is dependent upon nothing and nobody for existence. As such, he is over and above everything. He is distinct from the universe, living outside space and time, and unrestricted by them.

(b) While separate in being from the universe, his presence fills and permeates it.

(c) God is totally unchangeable in every aspect of his being.

L Loving

The essence of God's character is love and selfless kindness. He cares for all his creation and desires the ultimate good of the universe, especially of human beings.

C Creator

By his own choice, in perfect wisdom, and by his unlimited power, God has brought all reality outside himself into existence. As the Creator he is the rightful ruler of the universe and is perfectly equipped for this task with a morally flawless character.

O One, Omniscient

(a) There are not two gods or many gods. There is only one true God. God's name is plural, as there are three distinguishable persons within a single Godhead. As we conceive reality as matter, space, and time, distinct and yet inseparable, so the one God consists as Father, Son, and Holy Spirit.

(b) God knows everything; so he can never learn new information. He knows the past, the present, and the future. Time relative to one who is timeless is not time at all.

G Good

God is good. There is no mixture in his character. He is forever and unchangeably good. Because God is good, he is just and true. Everybody is accountable ultimately to him. This is whom I mean when I speak of God. This is not a random selection of attributes pulled out of the air. This definition reflects the conviction of millions of people throughout known history and represents the belief of the largest religious grouping the world has seen thus far.

For the purposes of this book, when I speak of God I am referring to him as revealed in the Bible, which is, I believe, the greatest book in existence and the oldest teaching about God. It is not my purpose in this book to critique other world religions or philosophies about God; if the Bible is true, and if Jesus is who he claimed to be, the conclusion on this point becomes inescapable. Christianity and other beliefs about God may appear superficially similar, but they are actually fundamentally different. They cannot all be true at the same time. If Jesus and the Bible are the final truth, then contradictory claims are false. More hard evidence for the reality of the God of the Bible will be presented as we look at how he has spoken and acted in history. Now, however, having defined what I mean by God, I want to present two simple, plain evidences for his existence.

THE VOICE OF GOD IN THE SOUL

The Russian writer and thinker Fyodor Dostoyevsky in his classic novel *Crime and Punishment* tells the story of a young man who rejects the existence of God. This young man murders an old woman. Believing there is no righteous God who will judge, and therefore no absolute standard of right and wrong, he knows that he should not feel guilty. However, he is consumed with a sense of guilt until he confesses his crime and hands his life over to God. It seems that there is truth forced upon us long before we encounter any theoretical knowledge or argument in life. This is called intuitive or a priori knowledge, truth obvious to every one of us, truth that cannot be doubted. We are conscious of feeling moral obligation to do what is right and to avoid what is wrong. We have a deep sense that some of our thoughts, words, and actions are praiseworthy and that others are blameworthy. Each of us is inescapably aware that we are moral beings with moral character.

When we do things that we somehow know to be wrong, we feel a sense of guilt. We may try to escape that guilt by ignoring it or by trying to intellectualize it away, like the character in Dostoyevsky's novel, but the hunter is relentless. We are hunted down by our own conscience. We do not just feel this obligation; we understand it with our minds. People will often talk about having a sense of duty. We speak constantly about what other people "ought" or "ought not" to have done. We instinctively know what we ought and ought not to do. The only reason we can understand what we ought to do is because our conscience tells us!

We can never know that we ought to do something until we understand what is right. Why else do we have a duty to do anything? How else can we say that anything is right or that anything is wrong? Some claim that there is no objective standard of right and wrong and that we should all do whatever we feel like doing. However, this kind of subjective morality is never lived out consistently. The modern conviction "if it feels good just do it" always dies when people run into injury or injustice in which they have to suffer. Invariably they then call for justice the loudest. This sense of moral obligation is universal and is often referred to as moral or natural law. No human being seems to be born without it. Our legal system and courts of law depend upon the power of it, and society suffers when men and women suppress and violate it.

In his book *The Abolition of Man* C. S. Lewis illustrates the universality of the moral law by citing examples of moral conviction in diverse cultures and places throughout history.[10] Pointing to Egyptian, Babylonian, Indian, Jewish, Chinese, Roman, Old Norse, American Indian, Anglo-Saxon, Greek, and Australian Aboriginal sources, it can be clearly seen that natural law or moral obligation has consistently and universally gripped the human race.

Despite modern people's considerable effort to shake free from this apparent inconvenience—notably in the forms of materialism, atheistic evolution, fascism, and Freudian psychology—nothing has succeeded in destroying or silencing this voice of God in the soul. We still understand that murder is wrong, that we should not lie, steal, betray each other, or live a life of total selfishness.

The reality of these first truths, written on our conscience, is still as potent as ever. This moral obligation, which makes demands of us all, leads us to an inevitable conclusion, to an inescapable deduction:

This law within implies a law without. The existence of our moral nature and this moral law implies a lawgiver and a judge. The creator of our nature must also be a moral being. That being is God, who is both Creator and Judge.

We also find it difficult to resist the conviction that we are accountable for our actions. We sense that how we respond to our conscience is important because we shall have to answer for it one day. This is not a comfortable thought, but again it is a feeling that we carry with us. The fact that we feel accountable implies that accountability is part of our nature, and that there is a ruler who will hold us ultimately accountable.

In summary, what does our sense of moral obligation point to? It is simply this: We are all moral beings who have a conscience. This is a fact, even for the atheist, and any pretense to the contrary is dishonest. Our conscience places us under a moral obligation that we obey or disobey as each circumstance presents itself. We feel that we shall ultimately be accountable for all that we say and do, which is why we feel guilt when we violate our conscience, yet are often pleased or happy when we obey it. All this implies a moral governor who gives us a moral law; this governor is God! So the existence of God is demanded and implied by the very fact of our moral nature. The voice of God in the soul echoes the fact that there is a God.

This is a closely reasoned argument that has been used for many years in different forms to demonstrate, independent of any academic or theoretical knowledge, that God's existence is plain to us all by what we know about ourselves. To me, along with the Bible's history, this is a most compelling argument for God and one that can bring us beyond reasonable doubt.

THE LORD OF THE DANCE

I vividly remember what it was like as a child to have overwhelming questions running through my head about existence. Sometimes I would sit and think and try to get my head around why I existed at all, until my mind simply quit and went blank. Who am I? What is life? How did it begin? If life goes on after death, what is eternity? Surely even that must end? The one thing we cannot accept as children or rationalize as adults is that things just happen by themselves. In my family, like most others, lots of things happened inexplicably. Food went missing from the cupboards, rooms messed themselves up, fights were started by phantoms, dirty footprints appeared across the carpet on their own, and all sorts of things were broken by the invisible man! All of us when questioned by Mum or Dad usually denied responsibility. "I don't know! It wasn't me!"

Why did this reasoning never get us off the hook? Because people cannot accept that things happen by themselves—something causes them to happen. That room did not get messy by itself; something or someone messed it up. This is a rule of common sense and common knowledge; all events must have a cause. No reasonable person would dispute that. This is the source of the persistent questioning of a child who asks why. If one asks why enough times, eventually you either get back to God or you simply have to assert something like, "It just is; that's all" or "Because I said so." The latter response is rather unsatisfactory, and even reference back to God will often prompt the question, "But who made God?"

This fact is telling. What it shows is that our minds demand a principle often referred to as "cause and effect." Philosophers call it "efficient causality." We all notice that some things cause other things to begin to be, to continue to be, or both. A woman may pick up and play the violin. She is causing the music that we hear. If she stops playing, the music stops. This can be said of everything we do. Every event must have a cause. For example:

Statement: I have just knocked over my cup of tea.
    Question: Why?
    Answer: Because my arm knocked it over.
    Question: Why?
    Answer: Because my brain told my arm to move.
    Question: Why?
    Answer: Because electrical impulses moved the muscles as I willed to move my arm.
    Question: Why?
    Answer: Because that's how the body works.
    Question: Why?

If we go on like that, we either get back to God or we resort to something irrational. What exactly do I mean by that?

As we have said, our senses tell us that the universe is real and that our world is a system of events and changes. These events, like the music from a violin or the spilling of a cup of tea, cannot cause themselves—this would be absurd. Something causes them to happen. Think hard for a moment. Everything at this moment is caused to be by something other than itself. All those things that cause other things also need a cause. But what is causing them if everything at any given moment needs a cause? The only reasonable solution is that there must be a first cause that is uncaused, self-existent, independent, and eternal. A cause that is not dependent on anything else to be its cause. This must be God. He is not an effect of something else; instead, he is the ultimate cause of all other effects. God is not an event that occurs at a given time like everything else; he has always been and always will be.

Imagine that existence is a present given from Mr. Cause to Miss Effect and so on down the chain of receivers, like a game of Pass the Parcel for however long the music plays. Unless someone has the present to start with, it cannot be passed along the chain. If there is no God who exists by himself, with an eternal nature (the one with the present), the gift of existence cannot be passed down through the chain of creatures, and we shall never get it.

But of course we exist, are here, are alive, and have got it—which means God must exist. He is the only one who always had the gift to give; it was not passed to him by anybody. This is the answer to the child's question, "Who made God?" For even a child knows that the gift of life came from someone and was passed to all from somewhere. So doesn't that include God? God by definition is the giver of the gift. No one made God, for God by his very name is the only one who just is! He is the great assertion, the only one who can truly say, "Because I said so."

The Bible begins with that very assertion: "In the beginning God." It does not argue about it or seek to persuade the reader by clever argument that it is true. It is simply stated. Human consciousness nods its head to this fact—*God is!* This is a constant theme in the Bible. It tells us that people intuitively know they have been given the gift of life from the giver of life who is eternal. King Solomon, famed for his wisdom, wrote, "He [God] has planted eternity in the human heart, but even so, people cannot see the whole scope of God's work from beginning to end" (Ecclesiastes 3:11, NLT). The Lord of the dance, the one who gives life to and sustains everything, has placed in the human heart a sense of immortality. Despite the fact that we cannot understand or explain an infinite, self-existent God, a persistent awareness that he is the source of all life remains embedded in the very essence of what it means to be a human being.

DO YOU WANT TO BET?

At the beginning of this chapter, I said that conclusive philosophic proof cannot be offered to decide the question of God's existence. This does not mean that it is perfectly reasonable to reject God's existence. The law of gravity cannot be "proved" as such, but that does not make it reasonable to jump from a tower expecting to fly. I believe the two plain, logical arguments I have discussed, quite apart from the unique revelation of the Bible or the life of Christ, put the case beyond reasonable doubt.

You may feel unconvinced by what you have read so far. This is understandable and has to do with my limited ability, not an absence of evidence for God. However, it is worth considering a final thought before going on. As people we often make decisions by weighing conflicting possibilities. For example, I need to go out. The clouds are gathering, and it looks like rain, but I don't want to carry an umbrella. It will be tiresome, and I may leave it somewhere. And it might not rain, and then I've carried it for nothing. So I set off without it. The skies open, and I get drenched. Why did I not just pick up the umbrella? I would have lost nothing by being prepared.

Similarly, Pascal suggested to those unconvinced by arguments about God's existence that they should take up his "wager." He encourages them to continue seeking and not to be lazy in this vital matter. He asks us, "Where will you place your bet?" If you place it in the existence of God and determine to seek him, you lose nothing, even if it turns out that God does not exist and there is no life after death after all. But if you bet against God and abandon searching for him, and he does exist and rewards those who seek him, you lose everything! Pascal's solution is simple: Bet on God!

> Since a choice must be made, we must see which is the least bad. You have two things to lose: truth and happiness. You have two things at stake: your reason and your happiness. And you have two things to avoid: error and misery. Since you must necessarily choose, your reason is no more affronted by choosing one rather than the other. How about your happiness? Let us weigh up the gain and loss in calling heads that God exists. If you win, you win everything. If you lose, you lose nothing. So do not hesitate; wager that God exists.[11]

This may at first appear rather clinical, but it should be looked at in the following way: If God exists and is the Creator of the universe who is infinitely good and true, then I owe him my love, obedience, and faith. To reject him, ignore him, and live as though there is no God would be to do unthinkable injustice to God and the entire universe. This is neither an argument for God's existence nor an attempt to force people to believe, but it should cause us to pause if we are tempted to stop seeking the truth. Those who never seek never find—an unreasonable and unhappy place to be. The Bible on the other hand offers this encouragement: "Anyone who wants to come to him must believe that there is a God and that he rewards those who sincerely seek him" (Hebrews 11:6, NLT).

Anyone can say a prayer to God. If we can sincerely say, "God, if you are real, please show me who you are," we are taking a wager that the Bible says God accepts and will respond to! To seek God will never be a waste of time and can take us far beyond reasonable doubt.

3

The Science of Belief

Life, even in bacteria, is too complex to have occurred by chance.

HARRY RUBIN,
PROFESSOR OF MOLECULAR BIOLOGY AND RESEARCH
VIROLOGIST, UNIVERSITY OF CALIFORNIA, BERKELEY

TALE OF THE UNEXPECTED

Let me begin this chapter by telling you a story. Are you sitting comfortably?

Once upon a point of infinite density, Nothing that was Something went boom. Then there was Everything. Everything eventually named Something Matter, the tragic character in our story. Sadly, Matter had no mind; yet this makes our tale all the more amazing!

Now Matter had only one companion, the hero of our fable, a mysterious stranger of unknown origin called Chance. Chance, though blind, was a brilliant artist. Chance taught mindless Matter to paint, and paint our pupil did. Matter painted a universe from center to rim on the canvas of a vacuum. And lo, innumerable galaxies emerged, filled with infinite wonders, beauty, order, and life. The inspired brush strokes of ignorant Matter, guided by the hands of blind Chance, created a cosmic masterpiece.

But as Matter and Chance were working away, they failed to spot our villain called Time. Time crept in unnoticed back at the boom and was extremely wound up about being stirred from his sleep. Time determined there and then to wind down again and thus rub the masterpiece out—as soon as he got hold of that Chance! Chance, being blind, didn't see Time coming, and mindless Matter was helpless to intervene.

Now Time ruins the painting little by little and brags that by Chance, it's just a matter of Time before the canvas is blank and the boom will swoon and everything that was Something will be Nothing again, once more a pointless point of infinite nothingness, with no Time for Chance to matter anymore.

The moral of this story, dear reader, is that there isn't one. For in the end everything means nothing at all and so there can be no morals. Ultimate meaning, value, and purpose are a dream—that is the message of this tale. My story is as empty as Matter's mind. Sadly, no one has ever been able to understand or communicate with the silent entities in our fable; they are, after all, merely constructs of subjective language. Yet, if the story has a meaning, they can never tell us, and soon we will be able to inquire no longer. As Shakespeare aptly put it, "Life . . . is a tale, told by an idiot, signifying nothing."

A REALITY CHECK

My rather depressing story is not just a sardonic play on words; it represents what we are left with if our universe is in fact Godless. It illustrates a view of reality that many atheists often put forward as credible and to their mind "true." In our last chapter we examined some evidence for the existence of God. We saw that it is rational, logical, and morally preferable to hold that God exists. But if we decide to reject that notion, we must be prepared to face the consequences. More than that, we must be able to satisfy ourselves that random chance is the cause of everything, and that this idea makes sense of reality and the experiences of our everyday lives.

There is no question that the doctrine of "random evolution" is one of the most common objections raised against the existence of God in our modern world. If, after all, it can be demonstrated that we arose by pure chance in cosmic chaos, "from the goo, through the zoo, to you," then we can eject God from our thinking altogether. In this chapter and the next we shall look at whether it is possible to be satisfied by the evidence for the spontaneous, random evolution of the universe and will carefully examine some of the practical and ethical implications that a chance universe holds for us as ordinary people.

FACT AND FICTION

I well remember my school days and the content of my "scientific" education. Certainly the overriding impression was that macroevolution (fish to philosopher, grand-scale evolution) was the epitome of good science. In fact, evolution for my geology teacher was inseparable from science itself. No alternative hypothesis was ever put to us, and any suggestion of a Creator was met with scorn.

In my vocation I have the opportunity to speak to many people, from teenagers upwards, and have discovered that my own experience in this is commonplace. Even in academic circles, where we congratulate ourselves on our educational freedom, naturalism is all too often assumed to be true, and people are consistently kept in the dark by a biased scientific establishment. Yet Darwinian evolution in all its current modes is only a hypothesis and one that, as we shall see, is in considerable scientific trouble.

The reasons for the widespread assumption of fish-to-philosopher evolution as established fact are involved and yet predictable. History is full of shattered theories that have resisted the hammer of truth for decades, even centuries, despite the accumulation of significant evidence against them. These dubious "facts" are usually last to fall among the general public who are often misinformed and therefore misled by the prevailing dogma. Statements concerning macroevolution, such as "The theory is about as much in doubt as [that] the earth goes around the Sun," made by atheist Richard Dawkins,[1] illustrate the point. Not only is this statement evidently false, it is profoundly antiscientific! There was a time when nearly all thinkers and scientists believed the universe was geocentric; to question this was tantamount to throwing away your brain and being regarded as a fool. It took years of scientific labor to overturn this false assumption.

All scientific theories by definition must be tentative and open to change as new evidence comes to light. If the scientific community makes a "physical theory" into a self-evident "truth," there is no point in having to establish its validity empirically. It then becomes anti-science and a fixed box into which all evidence must be fitted.

A recent discovery reinforces the fact that all scientific hypothesis must be tentative. Jonathan Leake, the science editor of a national newspaper, writes:

> The speed of light is not what it used to be. Scientists have discovered that light may once have travelled many thousands of times faster than now, posing new questions about Einstein's theory of relativity, which forms the basis for much of our understanding of the universe.[2]

It seems that the speed of light in a vacuum (299,798 kilometers or 186,291 miles per second) may not have been constant after all. Jonathan Leake continues:

> If the new hypothesis is right, the implications would challenge many modern 'laws' of physics. . . . The new theory has won tentative support from other astronomers. Dr John Ellis, senior theoretical physicist at Cern, the European particle physics research centre said: 'Einstein's work was a stepping stone to something more consistent with what we observe in the universe.'[3]

There is little doubt that the constancy of the speed of light was previously held as more likely a true fact than spontaneous, self-causing biological evolution; yet even this Einsteinian edifice is now in question. We dare not build our lives on the assumption that such and such a scientist, lecturer, or teacher who said this or that must be right. We should weigh the arguments responsibly but must never place a blind faith in the royal "they who say," for under inspection the validity of many statements made by scientists is doubtful, to say the least. There are reasons why people make these statements, and largely those reasons don't turn out to be unbiased or neutral. As Dr. Thomas Dwight of Harvard has observed, "The tyranny in the matter of evolution is overwhelming to a degree of which the outsider has no idea."[4]

DINOSAURS AND DIGITAL PHONES

Given that the evolution hypothesis is constantly evolving itself, what should we believe about evolution? Is it synonymous with pure science? Although some scientists will argue that as scientific conjecture macroevolution is conceivable, the idea that it is one of the established truths of science (if there is such a thing) is simply not true.

Modern science generally operates in two broad categories: operational science and ongoing science. The first concerns our present observations and technological progress. The last fifty years have been relentless in bringing us quicker, smaller, and faster operational gadgetry. Computers, space shuttles, satellites, and mobile phones all fall into the category of operational science, where we increase our understanding of how to manipulate for our use certain material elements (such as silicon chips). However, ongoing science, which hypothesizes about the past, is very different. The two functions of science cannot be regarded in the same way.

As an example, we do not blast people into space based on a doubtful hypothesis that the rockets will work properly—the technology is first rigorously tested and proven. But how the universe began, the origin of our space-time continuum, and how people came to be on Planet Earth is not testable in the same way. Much of the popular confusion with regard to "science" lies in confusing these two areas of investigation and giving them the same weight. "My mobile phone works brilliantly," we say, as does my e-mail and Palm Pilot (most of the time!). So when the BBC screens *Walking with Dinosaurs* and talks as though it is a known fact that the earth is billions of years old, during which time life spontaneously evolved from a primordial soup, we assume that these assertions must work equally well scientifically—but they do not! As these assumptions are so frequently heard, they appear authoritative. Add to that the deep voice of the narrator and the impressive computer graphics and we are convinced. Yet the evidence for these claims is often weak and unclear.

IN PRINCIPLE

Scientific knowledge has limits. The things we state with confidence because they are accepted today may not be so tomorrow. Science is essentially a tool for acquiring knowledge about realities. It seeks to investigate and describe as best it can what exists and arrive at objective facts based on observation.

Every theory in science requires basic assumptions that cannot be proved (as discussed in the previous chapter), and all investigation proceeds from these assumptions. These are metaphysical (beyond physics) assumptions, and each of us nurtures them in one form or another. Thus we do not have to reject science in order to have beliefs. In fact, we must all believe certain things before we can speak of science: for example, the belief that the universe can be rationally understood and that our minds are giving us reliable knowledge. Even by analyzing nature we attribute to ourselves a kind of supernatural status. If we were merely a part of nature, could we really stand back from it to classify it? If we were merely "part of nature's tapestry," we would not know it! Just as a dog does not ask why it is not a bear or a brick, we would not ask what it means to be human, what is right and wrong, where we are from and where we are going. We would be as unquestioning as a lark that sings with the sunrise.

All of our "science" proceeds from assumptions that seem plausible to us. Empirical science, therefore, has nothing absolute about it, and we would do well to remember that. Karl Popper has illustrated it well for us:

> The bold structure of its theories rises, as it were, above a swamp. It is like a building erected on piles. The piles are driven down from above, into the swamp, but not down to any natural or given base; and when we cease our attempts to drive our piles into deeper layers, it is not because we have reached firm ground. We simply stop when we are satisfied that they are firm enough to carry the structure, at least for the time being.[5]

In the light of that, my well-meaning schoolteacher who confused naturalistic evolutionary conjecture with science itself profoundly misunderstood the nature of scientific knowledge.

SILENT WITNESS

The idea that physical evidence speaks for itself is a fallacy. It must be interpreted according to a framework or worldview. Within this framework we theorize about the past and seek to gather evidence that will support a given hypothesis. The debate between naturalistic evolutionists and those who hold to creation (intelligent design) is primarily a dispute between two worldviews. The naturalist wears one set of interpretative spectacles, the creationist another. The naturalist believes that things made themselves, that there has been no intervention of God, and as there is no God, he has given no knowledge concerning things in the past. This is usually referred to as *naturalism*. In other words, the naturalists' worldview assumes that everything in the universe can be explained through a closed system of material causes and effects, without reference to a Creator. The data collected through scientific inquiry is therefore filtered through this lens. Dr. Arno Penzias, who won the Nobel Prize for physics, writes concerning this worldview:

> Today's dogma holds that matter is eternal. The dogma comes from the intuitive belief of people who don't want to accept the observational evidence that the universe was created—despite the fact that the creation of the universe is supported by all the observable data astronomy has produced so far. As a result, the people who reject the data can arguably be described as having a religious belief that matter must be eternal. . . . Since scientists prefer to operate in the belief that the universe must be meaningless—that reality consists of nothing more than the sum of the world's tangible constituents—they cannot confront the idea of creation easily, or take it lightly.[6]

The creationist on the other hand, in line with his intuition and the observational evidence, holds that it is most logical to posit a Creator behind the universe. There has to be a first cause (uncaused cause), since nothing can create itself—and he interprets the evidence accordingly. Furthermore, it is reasonable to assume that such a Creator could reveal the events of the past should he choose to do so.

So we see that underlying this question of random evolution is a philosophical "belief" that must be acknowledged.

RANDOM SPECULATIONS

Without getting bogged down in scientific jargon, how might we summarize the central points of the grand-scale evolutionary hypothesis? What is it saying about the origins of life in this framework of naturalism? In layman's terms, evolution asserts that things created themselves and that things which "appear designed" required no intelligent designer.

> It [evolution and naturalism] includes these unproven ideas: nothing gave rise to something at an alleged big bang, non-living matter gave rise to life, single celled organisms gave rise to many celled organisms, invertebrates gave rise to vertebrates, ape like creatures gave rise to man, non-intelligent and amoral matter gave rise to intelligence and morality, man's yearnings gave rise to religions.[7]

Can we really rely upon this unproven yet pervasive idea? Is it something to count strongly against the existence of God or the claims of the Bible? Is it a coherent framework corresponding to the way things are, upon which we can build our lives as individuals and as a community? Before discussing evolutionism in more detail, it is important to ask whether we, as the public, are being given the relevant evidence available. Is the data being assessed reliably to test these two frameworks? Are non-evolutionary models given a fair hearing?

Non-creationist science writer Boyce Rensberger admits:

> The fact is that scientists are not really as objective and dispassionate in their work as they would like to think. Most scientists get their ideas about how the world works not through rigorously logical processes but through hunches and wild guesses.[8]

This is to be expected, of course. Scientists are only human after all, and sometimes a hunch pays off. But are hunches admitted to by the scientific community when questioned about their guarded hypothesis of macroevolution? Generally speaking, absolutely not! Evolution is often assumed as self-evident without so much as a foot-note concerning its problems. But in a refreshing moment of intellectual honesty Professor Richard Lewontin (a geneticist) writes:

> We take the side of science (naturalistic) in spite of the patent absurdity of some of its constructs, in spite of its failure to fulfil many of its extravagant promises of health and life, in spite of the tolerance of the scientific community for unsubstantiated just-so stories, because we have an a priori commitment to materialism. It is not that the methods and institutions of science somehow compel us to accept a material explanation of the phenomenal world, but on the contrary, that we are forced by our a priori adherence to material causes to create an apparatus of investigation and a set of concepts that produce material explanations, no matter how counter-intuitive, no matter how mystifying to the uninitiated. Moreover, that materialism is an absolute, for we cannot allow a divine foot in the door.[9]

This is an astonishing admission. But from a leading evolutionary scientist it makes absolutely clear what many philosophers, scientists, and laypersons have been saying for years—evolutionism is an entrenched dogma that has been so jealously guarded that it is practically immune to all criticism, scientific or otherwise. The supposed scientific key to the origin of humanity and the universe has itself become antiscience.

Consider the words of the scholar Dr. A. Custance, author of the ten-volume *The Doorway Papers*, fellow of the Royal Anthropological Institute and member of the New York Academy of Sciences:

> Virtually all the fundamentals of the orthodox evolutionary faith have shown themselves to be either of extremely doubtful validity or simply contrary to fact . . . so basic are these erroneous assumptions that the whole theory is now largely maintained in spite of rather than because of the evidence. . . .
>
> As a consequence for the great majority of students and for that large ill-defined group, "the public," it has ceased to be a

subject of debate. Because it is both incapable of proof and yet may not be questioned, it is virtually untouched by data which challenge it in any way. It has become in the strictest sense irrational. . . . Information or concepts which challenge the theory are almost never given a fair hearing. Evolutionary philosophy has indeed become a state of mind, one might almost say a kind of mental prison rather than a scientific attitude. . . . To equate one particular interpretation of the data with the data itself is evidence of mental confusion.[10]

Anyone taking the time to investigate this matter will quickly discover that at the very least, "scientific naturalism" is as much a "faith" as any religion. But is evolutionism a reasonable faith?

4

Fish and philosophers

[Darwin] has lost sight of the most striking of the features, and the one which pervades the whole, namely, that there runs throughout Nature unmistakeable evidence of thought, corresponding to the mental operations of our own mind, and therefore intelligible to us as thinking beings, and unaccountable on any other basis than that they owe their existence to the working of intelligence; and no theory that overlooks this element can be true to nature.[1]

A MASS OF ASSERTIONS

One hundred years ago the widespread acceptance of macroevolution (vast information gaining upward change) precipitated an intellectual revolution that has affected nearly every aspect of modern life and the way we think about ourselves. From anthropology to psychology and ethics, evolutionary thought has become all-pervasive. However, in recent years the serious problems with orthodox evolutionary theory have been increasingly acknowledged, and numbers of leading scientists have subjected it to thorough critiques. This has begun an intense debate over nearly all aspects of this resistant scientific edifice.

In his book *The Blind Watchmaker* atheist biologist Richard

Dawkins doubtless voices the opinion of many when he says that Darwin "made it possible to be an intellectually fulfilled atheist."[2] I would put it this way: Without random macroevolution as the foundation stone, atheism has no intellectual credibility—it is a house of cards. If evolution can be shown to be false or extremely doubtful, the atheist has no foundation for his worldview. Given the stakes, it is no surprise that the doctrines of Darwinism have been, and still are, proclaimed with a fanatical fervency that shows questionable regard for the consistency of the evidence.

Interestingly, it is normally Christians who are accused of preaching dogma! However, Christianity and its tenets have been subject to immense scrutiny, detailed criticism, and vilification for two thousand years and yet remain standing, today commanding 1.6 billion believers. Since the second century, Christianity's apologists have brought its claims into the open, engaged objections, and, particularly over the last 150 years, countered the attacks of modernism. The average life span of a scientific theory is twenty years, but the Bible's message has remained. Whatever one thinks about that message, there is no denying the ceaseless investigation for credibility that the Christian faith has undergone. No other world religion has been subject to anything like this level of examination or so willingly laid itself open to scrutiny.

This, however, has not been the case with evolutionism. Its assertions are plentiful, but putting its claims and assumptions under the microscope is seen to be tantamount to heresy!

Darwin's own scientific contemporaries considered his work to be full of conjecture and low on hard evidence. In 1872 an attempt was made to elect Charles Darwin to the prestigious zoological section of the French Institute, but this failed because he received only fifteen out of forty-eight votes. One of the prominent members of the Academy gave the reason:

> What has closed the doors of the Academy to Mr Darwin is that the science of those of his books which have made his chief title to fame—the 'Origin of Species' and still more the 'Descent of Man' is not science, but a mass of assertions and absolutely gra-

tuitous hypothesis, often evidently fallacious. This kind of publication and these theories are a bad example, which a body that respects itself cannot encourage.[3]

Six years later he was elected a corresponding member in the botanical section of the same French Institute—a field about which he admitted he knew nothing!

The attraction of Darwinism, ejecting God from the universe, combined with humanistic philosophies, logical positivism, and existentialism, produced a cocktail of atheistic thought that flourished in the disillusioned soil of the twentieth century. But ironically, as Aldous Huxley once put it, "Facts do not cease to exist because they are ignored."[4] The popularity of evolutionary thinking does not change the facts. Have they changed since Darwin's own peers assessed his work? It would seem not. The Australian molecular biologist and researcher Michael Denton, a known critic of Darwinism, writes:

> [Evolutionary theory] is still, as it was in Darwin's time, a highly speculative hypothesis entirely without direct factual support and very far from that self-evident axiom some of its more aggressive advocates would have us believe.[5]

Let us take a brief look at just a few of the problems with evolutionary thought.

EX NIHILO

When thinking about the issue of evolution, most people immediately talk about monkeys becoming people and the possibility of finding the "final piece" of the puzzle, the "missing link." This shows the level of ignorance common today with regard to this whole subject; actually the problems start much further back than the imaginative "ape men" drawings of our school textbooks.

The first problem is that of the origin of the universe. Before we even consider by what means inorganic matter produced life in all its complexity, we must ask where all the raw material came from. (It is important to understand what naturalists are asking us to believe and on what basis they ask it.) One of the foundational principles of science is cause and effect. Everything must have an efficient cause. But the common belief and undoubted observation that "from nothing, comes nothing" is nonchalantly abandoned by the materialists' explanation for the origin of the universe.

The first law of thermodynamics tells us that the total quantity of energy in the universe is a constant. Isaac Asimov called this "the most powerful and most fundamental generalization about the universe that scientists have ever been able to make."[6] If the universe is a closed system of material causes, then it is impossible that the "entity" supposed to be the source of a "creative explosion" could have come into being from nothing!

Moving away from "steady state" and "oscillating models" of the universe, the most popular hypothesis has become widely known as the "big bang," which at least acknowledges the universe had a beginning. Billions of years ago—so the story goes—all of the matter and energy in the universe was condensed in a ball of subatomic particles and radiation, with a diameter smaller than a single electron (less than a pinhead). Its heat and density were of unimaginable proportions. No one knows how this ball came into existence, but for some reason it exploded. It expanded and cooled so that hydrogen and helium gas could be formed. This ether continued to expand outward forming the vast reaches of the universe until pressure and temperature dropped sufficiently. Eventually, through powers and means untestable and unknown, stars and galaxies formed, our solar system appeared, and the rest is paleontology!

Edward Nelson, Professor of Mathematics at Princeton University, comments, "In my view the big bang theory has been too widely accepted on the basis of insufficient evidence."[7] He believes that we do not even have a thoroughly established cosmology, never mind a coherent view of the origin of the universe. Robert Oldershaw observes, "In the light of these problems, it is astounding that the big bang hypothesis is the only cosmological model that physicists have taken seriously."[8] Astounding though it is, the big bang is widely adhered to, while the reality of the situation is that we have no coherent idea what happened at the beginning of the universe, and no way of knowing what physical laws may or may not have been in operation. The first law of thermodynamics rules out a matter-creating big bang because it violates the physical laws of energy conservation. Some scientists have tried to get around this by saying that these physical laws somehow do not apply at the "big bang"—an event where physical laws break down. Why? No scientist can tell us.

There are, of course, plenty of speculations as to how this ball of matter-energy arrived and subsequently exploded. One idea is that the big bang originated from a "quantum fluctuation of the vacuum." Now we are not all rocket scientists (me included), but because this is currently the popular view, it is worth a mention. In case any scientific reader should suggest that I'm glossing over the facts, I shall allow Dr. Wanser, Professor of Physics at California State University, to state them. Dr. Wanser has published over thirty reviewed technical articles and holds seven U.S. patents. In 1996 he was the recipient of the School of Natural Sciences and Mathematics Outstanding Research Award. In response to this speculation he writes:

> . . . in all experimentally observed processes involving elementary particle and nuclear reactions, something called Baryon number is conserved. The conservation of Baryon number ensures that when particles are brought into existence from energy, they occur in equal numbers of matter/anti-matter pairs. Thus in pair production, an electron and positron are produced, similarly, a proton and antiproton are produced.
>
> On the other hand, as far as we are able to observe, the universe appears to have an extreme dominance of matter over antimatter, which contradicts the notion that a big bang produced the matter that we see in the universe around us.[9]

In response to this, some particle physicists have proposed "Grand Unified Theories," which hypothesize equations that violate Baryon number conservation to make the matter/anti-matter problem fit. However, all experimental efforts have failed to support this. "The fact that there is no experimental evidence for violation of Baryon number conservation strongly calls into question any Big Bang scenario for the origin of matter in the universe."[10]

BOOMING AMAZING

Though it is difficult to grapple with some of the issues raised by physics because of the specialized language, please do not be blinded by science. Much claiming to be "scientific knowledge" in this area is sold to the public, virtually as fact, and does easily blind the uniniti-ated. The big bang falls into the domain of highly speculative theo-retical physics and is unsupported by many known physical principles, plus the observational data of astronomy. For example, matter distribution in the universe. In my view, a random universe-creating explosion remains a fairy tale for materialists.

Think about it. How did an explosion produce the finely tuned, ordered galaxies, solar systems, moons, and planets? Since when did explosions produce mathematically perfect accuracy? The great weak-ness of the big bang is that it simply cannot account for or explain the sheer number of complex condensed galaxies and stars within the uni-verse. Explosions throw matter apart; but we are asked to believe that this explosion produced the opposite effect of an explosion and brought matter together in the form of galaxies. Galaxies spin so fast that we cannot even understand why they do not just fly apart. Super-clusters of galaxies are linked together gravitationally in patterns thought to stretch half a billion light years. The M13 globular star cluster contains an estimated one million suns. Naturalists simply cannot explain how the big bang could have formed the intricate sys-tems we observe. Furthermore, astronomers estimate that as much as 90 percent of the universe could be made up of an invisible "dark mat-ter" of unknown makeup. British astrophysicist David Wilkinson comments, "It is somewhat humbling to realise that for all our dis-coveries we still do not know what 90% of the universe is made of."[11]

What is needed when confronted with all this is a degree of humil-ity in the face of what exists. The more we discover, the more we real-ize how little we know, as a whole new frontier of unsolved questions confronts us. Our human pride insists on throwing God out of the universe because we have made a large telescope and a powerful microscope. Though many once-treasured theories now lie aban-doned with the fashions of yesterday, we still present dubious theories as fact, because it suits us morally to discard God as "unscientific."

What will it take for us to see that this universe does not conform itself to our ideas, that we are not the conductors of the cosmological orchestra?

Stephen Hawking writes:

> Today scientists describe the universe in terms of two basic partial theories—the general theory of relativity and quantum mechanics. They are the great intellectual achievements of this century.
>
> The general theory of relativity describes the force of gravity and the large-scale structure of the universe (that is the structure on scales from only a few miles to as large as a million million million million miles—the size of the observable universe). Quantum mechanics, on the other hand, deals with phenomena on extremely small scales, such as a millionth of a millionth of an inch. Unfortunately, however, these two theories are known to be inconsistent with each other—they cannot both be correct.[12]

It would seem we have not explained everything after all. Our greatest theories are in disagreement—the two great intellectual achievements of the twentieth century are inconsistent with each other! What does all this boil down to? In short, we are dealing in guesswork. There is nothing wrong with guessing, of course, as long as we acknowledge it is just a guess!

Various other involved discussions could be made, but they fall outside my purpose here. What I am trying to highlight is that the spontaneous evolution of the solar system via a random big bang is so far a story without direct factual support. It requires a degree of faith that, in my opinion, goes far beyond that needed to embrace the logical and intuitive understanding that the universe did not create itself but was designed and created by God, in all its vastness, intricacy, and beauty. This is surely the more reasonable and scientific explanation. I shall leave the words of conclusion in this section to Roger J. Gautheret, former Professor of Cell Biology at the Paris Facility of Sciences: "I believe that notions such as infinite space and time, matter, structure, and order which govern the universe suggest the intervention of a spirit which has established the universe and its laws. Reflection on these subjects cannot avoid the notion of God."[13]

PRIMORDIAL SOUP OR SUSPECT STEW?

We cannot do justice to any discussion about origins until we have looked at the first great leap of molecular evolution. It is important to remember that if evolution has not taken place at one point in the evolutionary time line, it has not taken place at any. Evolutionism is a sequence of "events" all of which must occur to explain our existence. That begins with the spontaneous, random creation of the universe. If that took place, then the next step is that inorganic matter (non-life) had to give rise to life in a "primordial soup." I have tried to show that we are pushing believability in accepting step 1 of the process. Does step 2 look any more feasible?

How did life arise on this planet in the first place? Forget fish, mammals, and man—what about bacteria? Even granting that we have Planet Earth and an ocean, by what means did life come from non-life? Darwin himself clearly had no coherent idea about how it arose. However, in a letter he wrote in 1871, he imagined an environment he thought would be conducive: "if we could conceive in some warm little pond, with all sorts of ammonia and phosphoric salts, light, heat, electricity, etc. present, that a protein compound was chemically formed ready to undergo still more complex changes . . ."[14]

This notion soon took off, but the problems had been woefully underestimated, partly because at that time "spontaneous generation" (life developing all over the place in decaying matter) was still widely believed. Creationist Louis Pasteur later dealt the death blow to it by showing that air contained microorganisms that can multiply in water and therefore produce the illusion of spontaneous generation. In the early part of the twentieth century, accepting that Pasteur was right, other scientists proposed that perhaps, if you could just add billions and billions of years, the imaginary pond might indeed produce life. Thus was born the idea that nonliving chemicals can become living cells!

Now some of us will be scratching our heads, trying to remember what our biology teacher taught. Has it not been proved experimentally in a laboratory that life inevitably arose in a primordial chemical reaction? Unfortunately, this is the kind of misinformed "pop knowl-edge" being kicked around in restaurants, coffee shops, and univer-sity cafeterias that any informed biologist knows to be false.

In 1928 British biologist J. B. S. Haldane suggested that ultravio-let light acting on the earth's primitive atmosphere could have caused amino acids and sugars to concentrate in the ancient seas and would finally, given sufficient time, produce life. Dr. Stanley Miller of Chicago is the man now famed for seeking to test this experimentally. His results were published in *Science* magazine in 1953. Placing methane, ammonia, and hydrogen in a glass container with boiling water, he zapped the elements with a spark discharge device to simu-late lightning striking the supposed early atmosphere of earth. Amino acids (the building blocks of proteins and part of the basic substance of life) were formed after a few days. At the time this was hailed as a major breakthrough, but forty years later Miller himself was quoted in *Scientific American* as stating, "The problem of the origin of life has turned out to be much more difficult than I, or most other people, envisioned."[15]

Michael Denton states the matter more plainly:

> We now know not only of the existence of a break between the living and the non-living world, but also that it represents the most dramatic and fundamental of all the discontinuities of nature. Between a living cell and the most highly ordered non-biological system, such as a crystal or a snowflake, there is a chasm as vast and absolute as it is possible to conceive.[16]

The problems, then, are manifold, but they might be outlined in the following way: First, no one, including Miller, can know for cer-tain what the early environment of the earth was like. It is not deter-minable and therefore not reproducible. Second, according to the second law of thermodynamics, all organic material would degrade spontaneously with time, acting against any evolution of primitive life. Third, scientists agree that the presence of oxygen in the early atmo-sphere would prevent evolution because, according to organic chem-istry, it is impossible for the building blocks of molecules found in living things to arise in the presence of oxygen. But if there was no oxygen, there was no ozone layer; and without an ozone layer, the ultraviolet radiation of the sun would have destroyed any primitive life arising in the ocean. Fourth, all such experiments have triggered a chemical reaction generating only simple chemical building blocks, not the incredibly complex *information-carrying sequences* necessary for life, a gap difficult to overstate in its vastness. Finally, these experiments are anything but random, spontaneous processes.

These problems cannot be fully discussed here, but their significance requires that we look at them in a little more detail.

AMENABLE ACIDS

Miller had no grounds for assuming that the early atmosphere of earth was composed of ammonia, methane, and hydrogen. A favorable chemical reaction was needed; so an atmosphere with these gases was proposed. Miller has been contradicted in his view by NASA scientists since 1980; they believe that the primitive earth did not have these gases in any significant quantity, but was instead composed of water, carbon dioxide, and nitrogen. Experts now consider it impossible to get the same results with that mixture. Still others believe that the evidence points strongly to an early oxidized atmosphere on earth, precluding biological evolution as presently understood. Even by committed evolutionists, Miller's experiment is considered to be of little significance in the quest for life's origin today. To quote the late Dr. Wilder-Smith (a non-evolutionary scientist):

> . . . to state that . . . these amino acids which are formed by chance can be used to build living protoplasm is certainly grossly erroneous in principle, for they are for such purposes, in fact, entirely useless. Without exception all Miller's amino acids are completely unsuitable for any type of spontaneous biogenesis. And the same applies to all and any randomly formed substances and amino acids which form racemates. This statement is categorical and absolute and cannot be affected by special conditions.[17]

Synthesizing amino acids does not create life, and single-celled organisms are anything but simple! The difference, as already noted, between a living system and a non-living one is immense. Any living system must do at least three things: process energy, store information, and replicate. Human beings do this, as does bacteria, only more quickly. Non-living systems do not do these things. The intricacy, complexity, and ingenuity of the simplest single-celled organism exceeds the ability of our most advanced technology.

To build a living organism, the correct amino acids have to be isolated (twenty of eighty types are found in living organisms). They then have to be linked together in the right sequence to produce protein molecules. Many other molecules tend to react more readily with some amino acids than with other amino acids; so you have to remove them from the process. The issue is complicated by what is called "chirality." Amino acids must exhibit the correct chirality. If life evolved, all the amino acids involved must be of the "left-handed" form, since only the "left-handed" ones are found in living matter. For life to have evolved, not even the smallest amount of "right-handed" molecules could have existed in the primordial soup. Yet modern science knows of no means by which pure right- or left-handed forms can be formed through inorganic random processes. Laboratory experiments have produced "racemates" only—that is, 50 percent right- and 50 percent left-handed forms.

Such mixtures could not have given rise to life as we know it. Add to this the requirement that the protein molecules (at least two hundred of them) must be linked together in just the right sequence with the correct peptide bonds, all with just the right function to get a living cell, and you begin to get just a glimpse of the mind-boggling complexity of life.

All this is without touching on the even more complex problem of making DNA and RNA (information-carrying translation molecules). Klaus Dose of the Institute for Biochemistry in Mainz, Germany, stated that the complexity and difficulties in synthesizing DNA and RNA "are at present beyond our imagination."[18] Furthermore, we have absolutely no evidence of any "prebiotic compounds" that would allow any such process to occur. In the vast quantities of oceanic sediments available, if such compounds existed they would certainly have been found—but there is simply no sign of them!

MAGIC MATHEMATICS

If we now turn to the mathematical odds and probability of random evolution, things begin to get silly. The scientist Dr. Walter L. Bradley, author of *The Mystery of Life's Origins* and a widely respected expert in this field, says:

> The mathematical odds of assembling a living organism are so astronomical that nobody still believes that random chance accounts for the origin of life. Even if you optimized the conditions, it wouldn't work. If you took all the carbon in the universe and put it on the face of the earth, allowed it to chemically react at the most rapid rate possible, and left it for a billion years, the odds of creating just one functional protein molecule would be one chance in a 10 with 60 zeros after it.[19]

He cites a further example from the writing of Michael Behe to give a mental picture of what that means:

> The probability of linking together just one hundred amino acids to create one protein molecule by chance would be the same as a blindfolded man finding one marked grain of sand somewhere in the vastness of the Sahara Desert—and doing it not just once, but three different times.[20]

We are not able with our minds to comprehend such odds. The Nobel Prize winner and co-discoverer of DNA, Sir Francis Crick, states, "The origin of life appears to be almost a miracle, so many are the conditions which would have to be satisfied to get it going."[21]

SPACED OUT

Some scientists have therefore turned to the hypothesis of "biochemical predestination"—the idea that there is some inherent attraction causing life-forming amino acids to link up in the right sequence. But this is no help as it has been shown conclusively that the sequencing has nothing to do with chemical preferences. In what can only be described as desperation, other eminent scientists have proposed that life's original building blocks have come from outer space, somehow passing unscathed through the incinerating temperatures on entry into our atmosphere. Respected experts have in all seriousness turned to the idea that advanced spacemen from other planets planted life spores on Planet Earth as a cosmic experiment. At best this only raises the question of how life on other planets formed, getting us nowhere. More cynically we might ask whether such proposals do not simply show that the evolutionary cupboard is empty.

It is amazing, given the known facts contradicting the spontaneous origin of living cells, that the public in general, misled by a largely misinformed media, have swallowed it as an established fact. In a view directly supported by the factual data, it is increasingly believed that the random evolution of life on earth will prove to be the greatest hoax of the modern era. Because the meaning of the genetic code is virtually identical in all cells, as is the protein synthetic machinery, Michael Denton writes: "In terms of their basic biochemical design . . . no living system can be thought of as primitive or ancestral with respect to any other system, nor is there the slightest empirical hint of an evolutionary sequence among all the incredibly diverse cells on earth."[22] Klaus Dose sums up the situation for us:

> More than thirty years of experimentation on the origin of life in the fields of chemical and molecular evolution have led to a better perception of the immensity of the problem of the origin of life on earth rather than to its solution. At present all discussions on principal theories and experiments in the field either end in stalemate or in a confession of ignorance.[23]

Dr. Howard Byington Holroyd, retired head of the Department of Physics, Augustana College, Illinois, believes his own research has shown, "far beyond any reasonable doubt, that this theory [Darwinian evolution] is nothing more than physical and mathematical nonsense."[24]

THE MISSING LINKS

The greatest difficulty of all for a naturalistic view of the universe is rooted in step 3 of the evolutionary story. The highly implausible ran-

dom big bang and the strained notion of inorganic matter spontaneously coming alive is circumstantial compared to the hard evidence
in the rocks. The third step is the belief that single-celled organisms
gave rise to more and more complex life forms. That is, in one long
chain of transition through millions of years, every species alive today
or extinct in the past (including humankind) was the descendant of a
blob of protoplasm in the ancient oceans. This doctrine was nothing
short of a religious belief to Charles Darwin who, writing in the conclusion of his *Origin of Species*, attributes to natural selection (i.e., the
survival of the fittest and the elimination of the weak and deformed)
"moral goodness," acting for the good of being in bringing life toward
a state of bodily and mental perfection.

> As all the living forms of life are the lineal descendants of those
> which lived long before the Silurian epoch, we may feel certain
> that the ordinary succession by generation has never once been
> broken, and that no cataclysm has desolated the whole world.
> Hence we may look with some confidence to a secure future of
> equally inappreciable length. And as natural selection works
> solely by and for the good of each being, all corporeal and men-
> tal endowments will tend to progress toward perfection.[25]

We shall not spend time here discussing this flawed reasoning that
attributes intelligence, will, and moral awareness to the apparently
blind and random processes of evolution. We shall, however, note the
concept of an "unbroken succession of living things." Despite his elevated speculations Darwin realized that his theory was desperately
lacking in hard evidence—the fossil evidence in the rocks:

> Why is not every geological formation and every stratum full of
> such intermediate links? Geology assuredly does not reveal any
> such finely graded organic chain; and this perhaps is the most
> obvious and gravest objection which can be urged against my
> theory.[26]

Darwin recognized that the evidence for evolution would have to
come from the rocks, and that those who rejected his view of the fossil record would "rightly reject my whole theory."[27] If the fossil record

does not prove evolution beyond reasonable doubt, then evolution has surely not taken place.

I remember the detailed geological time line in my school textbooks and the beautifully illustrated progressions in diagram form as one species apparently evolved through a number of incredible changes into another altogether. Are these creative time lines and illustrations factual, or does the artist's impression give us the wrong impression?

The noted Canadian geologist William Dawson is unimpressed: "The record of the rocks is decidedly against evolution."[28] On what ground does he say this? He says it on the basis of what we know to be contained in the rocks. The fossil record is so discontinuous and the gaps so obvious that one wonders how evolution ever came to be regarded as credible. Darwin believed that the absence of a supporting fossil record would be rectified as more of the earth was explored and excavated. He was sure that with time a pick and shovel would prove him right. Darwin knew that if his hypothesis was right, "the number of intermediate and transitional links between all living and extinct species must have been 'inconceivably great.'"[29] The fossil record, however, shows the opposite.

Since Darwin's time the search for "missing links" has been nothing short of an obsession. The increased activity in the area of paleontology has been so immense that Michael Denton reckons 99.9 percent of all such research has been carried out since 1860.

> Only a small fraction of the hundred thousand or so fossil species known today were known to Darwin. But virtually all the new fossil species discovered since Darwin's time have either been closely related to known forms or, like the Poganophoras, strange unique types of unknown affinity.[30]

Denton goes on to point out that it is now a widely accepted fact that the "links" are simply missing due to the virtual absence of intermediate and ancestral forms.[31] To demonstrate this, I briefly quote some leading experts on the subject. The late aerospace engineer Luther D. Sutherland, in his work *Darwin's Enigma: Fossils and Other Problems*, cites interviews he conducted with five leading paleontologists from prestigious natural history museums around the world, all of which had extensive fossil collections. Sutherland records that "None of the five museum officials could offer a single example of a transitional series of fossilized organisms that would document the transformation of one basically different type to another."[32]

Along the same lines, two prominent scientists say:

> The known fossil record fails to document a single example of phyletic (gradual) evolution accomplishing a major morphologic transition and hence offers no evidence that the gradualist model can be valid.[33]

> It remains true, as every paleontologist knows, that most new species, genera, and families, appear in the record suddenly and are not led up to by known, gradual, completely continuous transitional sequences.[34]

As Denton puts it, "Simpson is admitting that the fossils provide none of the crucial transitional forms required by evolution."[35] The admissions speak for themselves. Dr. Colin Patterson, former Senior Palaeontologist at the British Museum of Natural History, states: "I will lay it on the line—there is not one such fossil for which one could make a watertight argument."[36]

In *Evolution Now: A Century After Darwin*, the Marxist and evolutionist Stephen Jay Gould acknowledges:

> The absence of fossil evidence for intermediary stages between major transitions in organic design, indeed our inability, even in our imagination, to construct functional intermediates in many cases, has been a persistent and nagging problem for gradualistic accounts of evolution.[37]

Supposed evolutionary transitions thus defy all belief. It is commonly held, for example, that whales evolved from land mammals. But whales have no pelvis. How could a land mammal with a shrinking pelvis support hind limbs, required for walking? Such a transitional form would be unsuitable for both land and sea and would therefore be extremely vulnerable; and what on earth would such a creature look like? We have no idea. The lowest known whales in the fossil record were completely aquatic from the first time they appeared.

Of course, these things are only a problem to evolutionists because they have already decided that evolution took place—it doesn't seem to dawn that perhaps, rather than looking for outlandish excuses for the absence of physical evidence, macroevolution has simply not happened. Certainly Darwin recognized that the fossil record would make or break his theory. Michael Denton writes:

> The fossils have not only failed to yield the host of transitional forms demanded by evolutionary theory, but because nearly all extinct species and groups revealed by palaenotology are quite distinct and isolated as they burst into the record, then the number of hypothetical connecting links to join its diverse branches is necessarily greatly increased.[38]

One of the most often cited "proofs" for evolution is the evidently fallacious development of the horse. Even the eminent paleontologist Simpson is forced to admit that "The most famous of all equid trends, 'gradual reduction of the side toes' is flatly fictitious."[39] There is little doubt that had the issue been one other than evolution, the theory would have been discarded long ago.

MONSTROUS PUNCTUATION!

The embarrassing lack of fossil evidence is tricky, to say the least. The only possible recourse would be to say that somehow the transitions have taken place without slow progressive change—they have, as it were, just happened suddenly. And indeed this was proposed back in the 1970s, an idea that has won some support. The abrupt appearance of life everywhere in the fossil record, fully developed, from plant life to the animal kingdom is popularly explained as "punctuated equilibria." This is proposed by Niles Eldredge and Stephen J. Gould, who suggest evolution has taken place in major creative episodes in different times and places, but with huge periods of stability in between. New species, then, have formed in those episodes during thousands rather than millions of years. This is often called the "lucky monster" theory.

Essentially Gould and Eldredge suggest that in order to generate new species (speciation), evolution massively speeds up and "punctuates" the normal tranquillity. However, this happens so quickly that these hypothetical transitions are not preserved in the fossil record. However you look at it, one cannot help feeling that this is all rather far-fetched and hugely convenient for the evolutionist. Even granting the plausibility of this accounting for the gaps that separate given species within a basic type such as a wolf and a fox, the idea that this explains the descent of a whale from a land mammal is very difficult to believe. Again Michael Denton writes:

> Such major discontinuities simply could not, unless we are to believe in miracles, have been crossed in geologically short periods of time through one or two transitional species occupying restricted geographical areas. Surely, such transitions must have involved long lineages including many collateral lines of hundreds or probably thousands of transitional species. To suggest that the hundreds, thousands or possibly even millions of transitional species which must have existed in the interval between vastly dissimilar types were all unsuccessful species occupying isolated areas and having very small population numbers is verging on the incredible![40]

This hypothesis does not remove the need for fossil evidence of transitional forms; it merely tells us why we cannot find any. The wide publicity of the idea did make many scientists aware for the first time of the flimsy nature of the hard evidence for evolution, exposing the "trade secret of paleontology": a lack of transitional forms in the record of the rocks. Darwin believed that any such sudden appearance of a new structure or organ would be a miracle, and the majority of biologists have agreed with him. Ernest Mayr comments:

> The occurrence of genetic monstrosities by mutation . . . is well substantiated, but they are such evident freaks that these monsters can only be designated as "hopeless." They are so utterly unbalanced that they would not have the slightest chance of escaping elimination through selection. Giving a thrush the wing of a falcon does not make it a better flyer.

Indeed, having all the other equipment of a thrush, it would probably hardly be able to fly at all. . . . To believe that such a drastic mutation would produce a viable new type, capable of occupying a new adaptive zone, is equivalent to believing in miracles.[41]

Do these things not in fact suggest that evolution is untenable? The Swedish botanist and geneticist D. Nils Heribert-Nilsson, after spending forty years trying to find evidence for the theory of evolution, considered the task impossible. In his 1,200-page magnum opus *Synthetic Speciation* he writes that the theory "ought to be entirely abandoned"[42] and that "a close inspection discovers an empirical impossibility to be inherent in the idea of evolution."[43] He offered a kind of secular creationism as an alternative hypothesis.

GOING BANANAS

You will notice that I have not commented on the "monkeys to men" issue so far in this chapter. The reason is, first, if evolution did not occur between reptiles and mammals, the notion of fish eventually becoming philosophers is irrelevant. Second, the apeman supposition falls prey to the same problems: No observations or experiments have ever demonstrated the process of human evolution. Marvin Lubenow, in his book *Bones of Contention*, points out that known skeletons (particularly skulls) either fall into an acceptable diversity of true humans (e.g., Neanderthals) or of nonhumans (e.g., the Australopithecines). The most often touted example of apemen are these extinct Australopithecines (southern apes). Research has shown them to be distinct kinds from the genus *Homo*. Analysis of the semicircular canals in their ear and the canal that carried the nerve to the tongue has demonstrated this. Evolutionary anatomist Charles Oxnard comments on these creatures:

> It is now recognized widely that the australopithecines are not structurally closely similar to humans, that they must have been living at least in part in the arboreal [tree] environment, and that many of the later specimens were contemporaneous, or almost so, with the earlier members of the genus homo.[44]

The DNA similarity between apes and people is often grossly exaggerated. Genetic differences are actually vast, and all arguments from DNA similarity are known by geneticists to be circular. As organic beings we share a great deal of biochemical similarity to organic life—even yeast! But arguments based on DNA similarity of any creatures are circular, as living organisms need to perform similar functions requiring similar structures (particularly apes and humans). The 2-4 percent of genetic difference between man and ape is so vast that it could fill forty large books. No matter how much evolutionists try to downplay the testimony of fossils, the simple fact remains: The fossil record cries out resoundingly against evolution.

DOODLING DNA OR DESIGN?

When all this is taken into consideration, we are thrown back to a crucial question: Are we the product of intelligent design, or perhaps the result of the blind doodling of DNA molecules in a contradictory, self-causing universe? No discussion of naturalistic evolution can be concluded without going to the epicenter of the issue.

The vital factor when looking at material structures is information. Information science is a discipline that affects all scientific inquiry. The assumptions of information theory enable us to reach conclusions and form the basis of our ability to understand each other, as the transfer of information is the fundamental principle of life. From a conversation with a friend, to the bee carrying pollen from one flower to another, there is constant information transfer.

Transmission of information requires:

• a physical carrier, whether a single gene or a human mouth;

• a defined coding system for representing ideas in the form of symbols, whether DNA letters or an alphabet-based human language.

A code is an intellectual concept (it does not have a material origin). The information in the code has a mental character, and all living organisms are based on complex coding systems.

The origin of the code is a huge problem for evolutionists because the physical carrier is not the information; it only carries the information—chemical codes written on molecules. Different levels characterize all information, in the same way that we might analyze a sentence in English. There is the grammar of the code, the meaning, the action prescribed, and the result. All of these categories appear to be nonmaterial.

Certain conclusions can be drawn from this. First, every piece of information requires the existence of a sender, just like receiving a letter in an understood language. Second, each piece of information is intended for a single recipient, like a personal letter, or for many receivers, like an e-mail to friends. Whether the Internet, with its physical network of cables, carries a message or whether writing paper and ink do it, neither the cables nor the computers, ink or paper are the information; they merely carry it. The code (language) of the message contains the information, which is useful, providing the recipient can interpret the language in which it is written. Information is inherently not a material entity; it is a mental or spiritual one. Material processes are not the source of information and cannot qualify as such. Whereas the movement of the keys on my computer as I write is the material process by which I am conveying information, the process is not the information. The information comes from the action of my mind, by my willingness to communicate in a code that can be interpreted (English).

At source, information is always established by the action of mind; so all information must have a mental or spiritual source. It therefore follows that information cannot be the result of chance probabilities. Mutation and natural selection, or a combination of law and chance, have not been shown to produce new coded information; they may shuffle, move, and lose existing information, but they cannot move information content essentially upward. If I gave you fifty bricks to build with, you could make different styles of structures but could not alter the number of bricks! Genetic copying mistakes (mutations) have not been shown to increase information content or functional complexity. If we record a music tape to another blank tape, we get a certain level of background noise on the copy. The copy is never as good as the original. Genetic mutations are like noise and produce various diseases, which are changes in genetic information. Such horizontal and downhill information changes, whether in antibiotic-resistant bacteria or human disease, are not evidence for grand-scale evolution. An unprofitable business slowly losing money, no matter how long it continues, will not finally make a profit!

This problem, when understood, is a serious theoretical objection to evolution because it challenges the possibility of a coded, information-generating natural (material) process, and therefore the theory of macroevolution fails. Evolutionists insist that only "material causes" can be considered in the science of origins, even for information, and this is where naturalism departs from the empirical laws of information science and objective science itself. When we consider that even the simplest organisms need "operational information" for a functioning system, and that the communication of information needs an understanding and agreement between the sender and the recipient already in place, we begin to grasp the complexity of intelligent design in the universe. We might summarize it in this way:

• There can be no information without a code.

• There can be no information without a sender.

• There can be no information without an original mental/spiritual source.

• There is no such thing as random information.

This can be illustrated by a remarkable story from the Second World War when the U.S. Marines employed the services of the Navajo Native Americans as "code talkers," and those Native Americans played a pivotal role in the Allied victory in the Pacific.[45] The Japanese were skilled code breakers who consistently cracked the codes of the U.S. Army during the war. But they failed to break the code used by the Marines. In 1942 the Marine commanders were persuaded that the Navajo language, only spoken in isolated parts of the American Southwest, would be the perfect basis for an unbreakable code. Navajo is an immensely complex language, with no alphabet or symbols, and consequently comprehensible only to those who have had extensive exposure to it. It was reckoned that only around thirty non-Navajos in the world spoke the language, and none of them were Japanese!

The Navajo recruits created the now-famed Navajo code. Their task was to transmit information about the battle (reports, battle plans, etc.) over the radio and the telephone. They were amazingly quick and effective. The code itself worked by each letter of an English word being transmitted as a Navajo word that, when translated into English, started with that letter. So any given letter could be represented by more than one Navajo word. The code proved unbreakable even for years after the war. Thousands of messages were sent without error.

Information does not arise by random processes but is guided by the action of the mind.

The Navajo code was not a random collection of noises (though it doubtless sounded like that to the Japanese), but a complex code containing vital information. There is no known documented example of information arising from a mindless natural process. As Dr. Werner Gitt, a leading information scientist, has put it, "There is no known natural law through which matter can give rise to information, neither is there any physical process or material phenomenon known that can do this."[46]

Noted physicist and evolutionist Paul Davies likewise acknowledges, "There is no known law of physics able to create information from nothing."[47] Let us grant for a moment the evolutionist's "primitive earth" and the first "protocell" developing the information coding to manufacture just one functional protein. This code would be as useless for producing life as the Navajo code was for battle information to the Japanese, unless the complex machinery that recognizes all of the DNA molecules' chemical letters was already in place (simultaneously translating them into the correct amino acids). Tapping into the Navajo transmission was easy enough, but knowing how to translate and apply the message was another matter. Without the knowledge of the language, the code was useless. The same is true with genetic information. The translation machinery itself is encoded in the DNA, a frustrating situation for evolution. Dr. Michael Behe summarizes:

> The conclusion of intelligent design flows naturally from the data itself—not from sacred books or sectarian belief. . . . The reluctance of science to embrace the conclusion of intelligent design . . . has no justifiable foundation. . . . Many people, including many important and well respected scientists, just don't want there to be anything beyond nature.[48]

MONKEY MORALS

Having examined some of the theoretical and evidential flaws in naturalistic science, we come to a closely related question: What are the ethical implications of evolutionary thought? When evolution is pushed to its logical conclusions, what does this worldview have to say about morality? Have we an example of evolutionary morality in action? If we do, what does it tell us about the all-important question of how we are to live? This is one of the most overlooked and neglected areas of inquiry today. Yet it is no idle question. In approaching ethics a simple fact must be stated, one that can be backed up in the starkest of ways in history: Ideas have consequences. What we believe will finally determine how we behave.

If we are merely over-evolved monkeys, then we may all make up our own morals. Evolutionists are normally humanists. To put it another way, the biological belief of all humanists is evolutionism. They are working toward a science of ethics based on atheism, naturalism, and evolution. Christians, on the other hand, base their ethics on the Bible's teaching and its worldview: God defines right and wrong. This distinction is the most important factor in ethical questions today, a distinction in which humanists rejoice.

Paul Kurtz, the author of the Humanist Manifesto II, states, "The traditional super-naturalistic moral commandments are especially repressive of our human needs. They are immoral insofar as they foster illusions about human destiny (heaven) and suppress vital inclinations."[49]

Two things are noticeable in this statement illustrating the great ethical divide. First, it is presupposed that the teaching of the Bible and Jesus Christ are an illusion—in other words, God does not exist and therefore cannot give commandments. And second, that biblical commandments are themselves immoral, as they limit the supposed human right of an unfettered pursuit of biological or psychological inclinations. Hence the same humanist manifesto is honest enough to admit in its preface that humanism is "a philosophical, religious and moral point of view."

The great problem for naturalistic ethics (humanism) is obvious. To phrase it philosophically, how can an ethical ought be derived from a biological is? How can the assumed fact of evolution be the basis for moral value judgments? If we say that some things that evolve are bad, on what basis are they bad? (One can only appeal to some external law, the very thing that they are trying to deny.) Many humanists admit that they can find no basis for designing an ought; they can find no real moral imperatives. If A evolved from B, one can only say A is different from B, not better or worse. But if there is no basis for determining right and wrong, how can we praise or condemn anyone's actions?

Furthermore, who will make the rules to govern society, and by what authority do they do so? If a government of "the people" in a totalitarian state is the answer (as in Marxism and communism), how can we determine what tyranny and oppression are? Can morality be dictated by a human government where inevitably some are "more equal" than others? In the democratic world we call laws good or bad, tyrannical or just, by intuitively assessing them on the basis of an external "felt" moral law. If a law does not correspond to our natural sense of justice, we consider it an unjust law. But if there is no determinable right and wrong, which is the consistent and logical position of evolutionism, then the Hitlers, Stalins, and bin Ladens of this world are innocent of any crime. This is the essence of the problem faced by evolutionists wanting to engage ethical questions. The evolutionary humanist is pressed to an inescapable conclusion: There are no absolute moral standards, and morality is merely the result of an interplay between evolution, tradition, and social convention, which can be altered, updated, and changed depending on the situation.

THE RIGHTNESS OF WRONG

Humanists consequently differ on almost every point of moral inquiry. Humanistic ethics is a mass of confusion. Any visit to the Ethics section of your local library will adequately demonstrate this. Humanists admit that an absolute moral law cannot rationally exist without God, but their difficulty is that they simply cannot agree on what morality apart from God really means. To be able to say that anybody ought to do something and ought not to do other things, one must refer to the existence of a moral law or ethic that dictates that ought. Otherwise, on what basis should we choose to do some things and not others?

For the naturalist, ethics are tied inextricably to biology in the evolutionary "hope of betterment." Through this process people may subjectively reason their way to the good on the upward curve of a humanistic dream. This is a wholly speculative idea, riddled with logical fallacies. But granting those dubious assumptions, where does the wedding of biology and ethics leave us? It leaves us without a moral law that exists outside the material world. Thus Darwin's concept of the struggle for existence becomes the new absolute upon which moral decisions are made. In his autobiography Darwin wrote:

> A man who has no assured and ever present belief in the existence of a personal God or of a future existence with retribution and reward, can have for his rule of life, as far as I can see, only to follow those impulses and instincts which are the strongest or which seem to him the best ones.[50]

If we are the product of meaningless chance mutation, if God is but an illusion and biblical commandments are essentially immoral, then the only real truth about reality is the ebb and flow of evolution. If the processes of chance are taking us on an upward curve of betterment (though there is no rational ground for it not to be a downward curve), then those who are honest will seek to aid that struggle for existence to ensure that only the "fittest" survive and go on to procreate—the meek inherit nothing in the evolutionary scheme. As one noted anthropologist and evolutionist has starkly put it, "The conclusion I have come to is this: the law of Christ is incompatible with the law of evolution. . . . Nay the two laws are at war with each other . . . and . . . the Sermon on the Mount is a condemnation of the evolutionary ladder."[51]

One result of this ethic is moral relativism, the generally accepted "morality" of the humanistic worldview. Certain actions are deemed moral for some and not for others, right at one time and wrong at others. All ethics become essentially "experimental acts" tested only by the results: a morality of self-interest, self-assertion, and self-preservation. "Does this action result in what feels good to me?" becomes the sole moral criterion. All dogmas restrict our so-called freedom (except the dogma that there is no higher law!); therefore a higher law is rejected as repressive. This makes some people unreachable and impervious to moral constraints.

Popular moral relativism, which asserts "absolutely" that all ethics are relative, is the comparatively tame consequence of evolutionary thought. An obsession with pleasure and self is the reaction of many in our culture to the rejection of the absolute moral commandments of God. Notably, popular relativism retains an inconsistent revulsion to evils it still considers unacceptable, like mass terrorism, murder, and rape. But the logical consequence of ethics based on evolutionary biology has two even more sinister aspects.

IT WASN'T ME; IT WAS GENE

Biological determinism becomes, and is indeed becoming, a dominant idea because it is a logical outcome of evolutionism. It seeks to excuse and to justify certain behavior on the basis that it must be genetically determined, instead of our moral actions being the result of free conscious choices. Given that evolution is an irresistible, deterministic force constantly working outside our direct control, a contemporary question in ethics has become, "How responsible am I for my actions?" If I have been cast forth by evolution with certain genetic predispositions, can I be blamed for my criminality? Can I control my sexual appetites? For example, some people now believe that one can be born homosexual. Two practices being studied by humanists are pedophilia and incest, as both are suspected of being "biologically determined."

This will eventually result in the disintegration of a rational legal system. I am regularly astonished by some supposed grounds for "diminished responsibility" based on certain doubtful biological and psychological theories. Instead of wrong actions being a crime, they are increasingly thought of as a sickness. Evolutionary thought in the nineteenth century led to the idea that criminals must have less developed brains, and this could be seen by the cranial form, jawline, and nose shape. This has since been proven ridiculous, but the new threat to the legal system suggests that people may be unable to help what they do because their DNA has caused them to act that way.

The frightening thing is that without an absolute moral law to discern right from wrong, how do we decide who is "sick" and who is not? If we are all to do what seems right and best to us (driven by our DNA), who is to say whether pedophilia is healthy or sick? If we are merely to follow our impulses, who is to say that rape is sickness? After all, other beasts need to propagate their species by the strong taking advantage of the weak! Have some not already said that moralizing Christians are the sick ones? That the Ten Commandments and the Sermon on the Mount are immoral? "They try to restrict sex and pregnancy to a lifelong marriage relationship—how sick and repressive!" Morality can quickly be turned on its head in a world that no longer obeys God. The new commandment from the men in white lab coats is, "You shall all follow Gene!"

THE FINAL SOLUTION

Some may be thinking that the foregoing is a preposterous exaggeration, an attempt at scaremongering. How could a civilized society ever accept such things? Surely enlightened people do not advocate making up their own rules? But the results are already with us. Humanist Max Hocutt, who denies God exists and consequently admits there is no moral law, has stated, "Furthermore, if there were a morality written up in the sky somewhere but no God to enforce it, I see no good reason why anybody should pay it any heed, no reason why we should obey it. Human beings may, and do, make up their own rules."[52]

Few have so clearly outlined and promoted the biological ethics of evolution as the influential twentieth-century figure Julian Huxley, brother of Aldous Huxley (author of *Brave New World*) and grandson of Thomas Huxley, Darwin's loyal supporter. Julian Huxley was a devoted evolutionist. A modern figure, he developed his evolutionary humanism as a complete system of belief in his best-known work, *Religion Without Revelation*. He received his degree in zoology from Oxford, where he later taught. He became Professor of Zoology at Kings College, London in 1925 and in 1946 was appointed Director General of the United Nations Educational and Scientific Organization. In 1952 he became President of the British Humanist Association and in 1957 was awarded the Darwin Medal by the Royal Society. In 1962 he was elected Humanist of the Year, and in 1973 he signed the Humanist Manifesto II. A prolific writer, he was one of the most influential evolutionary thinkers of the modern era.

Huxley referred to what he called the "gospel of evolutionary humanism." His basis for ethics was simple and logically consistent: Whatever aids the evolutionary process is good; whatever hinders it is evil. His faith was placed in human possibilities. A little book, perhaps less known, comprises a series of articles by Huxley first published in 1926. Originally written for a popular radio broadcast, these articles, entitled *The Stream of Life*, outline in lay terms his views on heredity and evolution, culminating in the final chapter, "The Hope of Betterment." Huxley, let it be remembered, was a respectable, educated Englishman who held prestigious positions throughout his career.

For Huxley, the human race is evolving upward, and our duty is to aid that process by "improving" the human stock. As highly evolved animals, we should consider human beings in much the same way as livestock and should employ selective breeding to ensure that "defective" stock do not increase and thus mess up the process. He believed that the differences in physical and mental ability, not just appearance in individuals, was due far more to heredity (genetic quality) than to environment and conditioning. He writes, "The important fact has been elicited that talent and genius are not on the average associated with low physique, nor with special defects like epilepsy . . . special talent in one direction is on the average correlated with high general all round ability."[53]

If you have not grasped the full force of what is being suggested here, consider the following from his final chapter:

> The Eugenic idea flows inevitably from a realization of certain simple facts. First and foremost is the fact of evolution, the realization that the inherited capabilities of man have developed by slow upward progress from those of brutes [animals], and that there is nothing whatever against the process being continued further in the upward direction . . . finally, the realization that the hereditary qualities of the nation are definitely if slowly being lowered, while in the past the pruning knife of natural selection kept the stock up to standard . . . we ought to try to ensure that

the children who are to come into the world shall have the best possible constitution; and this can be done by some control of the individual's right to bring children into the world.[54]

Huxley continues by outlining what any responsible eugenicist would propose for today:

> . . . that certain types of defective people should be prevented if possible from having children, and so from propagating the defect. Feeblemindedness is as much a disease as is scarlet fever or small-pox. We do not allow a small-pox patient to propagate his disease by coming into contact with other people. . . . There are around 400,000 mentally defective persons in these Islands. If we could prevent all of them from reproducing, the percentage of defectives would be halved in from three to five generations. Reproduction can be stopped by segregating defectives in special institutions, or by artificial sterilization—an operation that is trifling for men, though rather more serious for women, while the psychological effects, again especially in men, are negligible.[55]

He speaks also of our misguided sense of pity toward the handicapped:

> But what are we to think when pity for suffering individuals leads us not only to preserve them, but to allow them to reproduce and so not only to lower the quality of the race, but to produce more suffering in individuals yet unborn? What is one to think of the misplaced kindness which, to give an actual recent case, takes an epileptic woman to hospital to be operated on to remedy sterility; or the sentimentality which rejoices at the "happiness," so called, generated by the marriage of two deaf mutes?[56]

More examples follow to give you a clearer picture of his hope for humankind.

> What anguish to have an imbecile child, or to know that one is oneself afflicted with the taint of insanity! What waste to spend millions on the education and care of the feeble-minded, if the

result is another generation of feeble-minded to care for and educate![57]

. . . some action is imperative . . . when they [people] realize this, they will demand that the government, through the census or through a special department of state, such as that for race-biology recently established in Sweden shall take steps to acquire the needed knowledge; and we can be sure that, once the facts are there and the knowledge of them is widely diffused, action will follow.

Let us not forget that we men are the trustees of evolution, and that to refuse to face this problem is to betray the trust put into our hands by the powers of the universe.[58]

One is not exactly overwhelmed by the compassion or moral virtue of his words and proposals! These reflections remind one of the ideas of a certain fascist dictator in Germany whose actions precipitated the Second World War. By contrast, consider the words and actions of Jesus Christ when he met a deaf man unable to speak properly:

> He took him aside in private, away from the crowd, and put his fingers into his ears, and he spat and touched his tongue. Then looking up to heaven, he sighed and said to him, "Ephphatha," that is, "Be opened." And immediately his ears were opened, his tongue was released, and he spoke plainly. . . . They were astounded beyond measure, saying, "He has done everything well; he even makes the deaf to hear and the mute to speak."
> —MARK 7:33-37, NRSV

Ideas have consequences. If human life is not sacred, it is expendable. If we are mere brutes, then we can be bred for better pedigree like any dog. But let us be careful before we condemn Huxley as an extremist, for his program of eugenics is carried out today in many ways that we deem "responsible." The eugenic idea is that we do not allow "defective stock" to be bred. Today we abort millions of children, often on the basis of a "high risk" of some disorder, whether mental like Down's syndrome or physical like spina bifida. In many instances babies are aborted on suspicion of far less debilitating conditions, or indeed for no reason other than inconvenience. It is well known that people with all kinds of disability or abnormality, genetic or otherwise, can and do live fulfilled and productive, happy lives with no shortage of genius flowing through their veins. I'm sure the physicist Stephen Hawking would not have existed in Aldous Huxley's *Brave New World*. What gives us the right to determine who should live and who should die, who should reproduce and who should not? Evolution grants people every right, because absolute right and wrong in the biological struggle do not exist. Fit and unfit, the healthy and the sick—these are the new ethical criteria.

Today some women, as illustrated in an episode of the American comedy series *Friends*, can select sperm from a sperm bank and fish through a catalog to select a male specimen with the desired attributes and aptitudes. Perhaps most notably, genetic engineers are promising the future reality of selecting and isolating the desired genetic attributes, manipulating DNA in such a way that we could even choose our offspring's eye color, not to mention the sex and physique. These things are not in the domain of pure science fiction. As I write, the claim has been announced that scientists have cloned a human embryo. It is supposedly intended only for prevention of disease, not for production of children; but some scientists will proceed, regardless of what ethicists or governments might say. The world of the films *Gattaca* or *The Sixth Day* may not be far off, because we have hidden Huxley's eugenic ideas by shrouding them in the respectable cover of modern medicine. Did the Second World War really destroy the notion of the "Superman"? Not as long as the evolutionary fiction holds sway.

Many modern humanists (as in the case of Huxley) are intellectual snobs. Note how often Huxley referred to the "feeble-minded." Some of us are often considered a hindrance to the progress of humanity! People with below average intelligence, whom humanists claim to defend from the "oppressive moralizing" of Christianity, are all too often regarded with quiet contempt. As the leading humanist, Corliss Lamont, puts it, "For the Humanist, stupidity is just as great a sin as selfishness; and . . . the moral obligation to be intelligent ranks always among the highest of duties."[59] The implication is that only the "intelligent" are fit to determine right and wrong, and therefore to be society's moral guides. Ironically, they set up what they themselves claim to resent—moral guidelines that the rest of society should follow. As a humanistic philosopher once said to me in conversation, "Now that the idea of God is discredited and no longer taken seriously, *we* are developing a system of morality without reference to him."

Finally, there is no question that the inspiration for the Nazi regime in Germany was evolutionary ethics. Hitler and others openly proclaimed evolution as the inherent justification for their atrocities. Friedrich Von Bernhardi, in his work *Germany and the Next War*, wrote, "War is a biological necessity; it is as necessary as the struggle of the elements of nature; it gives a biologically just decision, since its decisions rest on the very nature of things."[60]

I have asked the question, have we an illustration of evolutionary ethics in action? The answer is, yes, several. Most notably in Nazi Germany and Communist Russia and China. Years ago Adam Sedgwick, the Cambridge geologist and colleague of Darwin, commented on Darwin's *Origin of the Species*: "[It is] a dish of rank materialism cleverly cooked up. . . . And why is this done? For no other reason, I am sure, except to make us independent of a creator."[61] He predicted that Darwin's ideas would herald a new era of brutality. History has proved him right. If space permitted we could talk about the estimated 110 million lives lost from 1917 to 1959 in the Soviet Union due to Marxist evolutionary ideology. The leaders of Communist China put to death in the region of thirty million. Multitudes have been slaughtered in Cambodia and other parts of Southeast Asia. About two billion men and women have been politically enslaved and denied their freedom because of Marxist ideology. In 1861 Marx wrote, "Darwin's book is very important and serves me as a basis in natural selection for the class struggle in history."[62]

Sir Arthur Keith and many historians of the period acknowledge that Darwin's doctrine of evolution bred war in Europe. In 1935 a committee of psychologists representing thirty nations issued a manifesto in which this was stated bluntly: "War is the necessary outcome of Darwin's theory."[63] Hitler sought to conform the practices of Germany to evolutionary theory. In evolution he found his great weapon against Christian values, which he vilified: "I regard Christianity as the most fatal, seductive lie that ever existed."[64] In *Mein Kampf* he wrote, "I do not see why man should not be just as cruel as nature . . . all that is not of pure race in this world is trash."[65] I challenge the reader who may doubt this connection to study the matter carefully. You will discover that evolutionary thought lies at the root of the horror of the Nazi dream. The historical philosopher John Koster leaves us with a clear warning:

> Darwin's and Huxley's picture of man's place in the universe prepared the way for the Holocaust. . . . Darwin the scientist directly inspired Nietzsche's superman theory and the Nazi corollary that some people were subhuman. . . . People have to learn to stop thinking of other people as machines and learn to think of them as men and women possessed of souls. . . . History doesn't need another one hundred million deaths to prove that scientific atheism is a form of mental illness.[66]

STARK CONTRASTS

I am not suggesting that all people who believe evolution to be true hold such ethics, or that all humanists are in sympathy with Nietzsche's and Hitler's philosophies. What I am saying is that if the evolutionist is to carry his "truth" about reality into the domain of ethics, he must at worst approve of Julian Huxley's eugenics and Hitler's Superman, or at best admit that he has no grounds on which to tell other human beings that they ought or ought not to do anything—the atheistic evolutionist has no binding moral laws.

Are we all just "dancing to the DNA" as Dawkins has put it, or are human beings more than amoral biochemical machines? Is there right and wrong and thus a moral absolute to guide our actions, or is such talk purely sentimental nonsense? It is said about the French atheist Voltaire that when his atheistic friends came over to dinner, they were forbidden from speaking about their atheism in front of the hired servants who waited on them. Voltaire was fearful that if they should hear such godless talk and become convinced of what was said, they might steal his belongings and murder him in his sleep. He realized that the moral law and belief in future accountability for our actions kept his hired hands from crime! Immanuel Kant memorably said that the moral law within filled him with "ever new and increasing wonder and awe."[67]

We simply cannot have a moral society without God; history has proved that. The Bible teaches that we are created by God in his likeness—moral, spiritual, and free—with his law of love planted in our consciousness. Jesus taught that, far from "dancing to the biological law of the DNA," we have God's law of love to obey that requires love both for God and for our neighbor. The apostle Paul taught, "In him [God, not DNA] we live and move and have our being" (Acts 17:28, NRSV). We are therefore infinitely valuable beings, created by God to know him.

As we move on to look at the Bible and its message, let us notice the contrast between humanism and the Christian view of the sanctity of life, and ask ourselves which principles we can build our lives on as individuals, as families, and as a community. As we consider the person of Jesus Christ, let us consider whether we should trust him or men like Darwin and Huxley and their successors, such as Dawkins, Gould, and Peter Singer. The humanist ultimately advises, "Be yourself; decide what is right for you; follow your own instincts." Christianity, to the contrary, says, "Obey and worship God, and follow the standard seen in Jesus Christ." C. S. Lewis has summarized it well for us: "There is nowhere this side of heaven where one can safely lay the reins on the horse's neck. It will never be lawful simply to 'be ourselves' until 'ourselves' have become sons of God."[68]

5

Echoes of Eden

The lover of money will not be satisfied with money; nor the lover of wealth, with gain. This also is vanity.
ECCLESIASTES 5:10, NRSV

Our life-long longing is no mere neurotic fancy, but the truest index of our real situation.
C. S. LEWIS

MOTORING MISERY

It was surely a day to be remembered. A day that would make an indelible mark on my life, a hiatus of happiness, certain to shine out as monumentally significant. I had dreamed about this day for several months. Just the thought of it had kept me going through the drudgery of the most soul-destroying work I had ever undertaken.

For weeks I had watched a conveyor belt of silver trays pass before my eyes. In front of me, just beyond the conveyor, still larger silver trays overflowed with a most unpleasant sight. To my right, cold, skinned chicken necks, in the center a mound of chicken livers, and to my left skinned chicken gizzards. This was the one machine on the vast factory floor of the "E line" (bar the gizzard skinner) that you couldn't wear gloves on; hence my hands sank into these piles of poultry foulness. As the small trays sped by, great dexterity was required to place one of each of the innards into every little tray. The trays then wound their merry way past my colleague who placed two further lumps of unpleasantness onto them until they finally reached a machine that tidily bagged the little goodies in plastic, ready to be shoved into the chickens. Yes, I was working on a giblets packing machine!

It is hard to describe the intensity of boredom I experienced working at that chicken factory. I remember getting the job as a stopgap earner after finishing my A levels [high school], before leaving for college. It was a sheer endurance test: seven hours a day on your feet in the same position, functioning like a robot. To keep myself mentally occupied, I would recite songs and passages of books to myself. Most of all, however, I would daydream about the day I was so looking forward to, the day that would revolutionize my young life—buying my first car! This was the only reason I was there, of course. I wanted to earn enough to buy the symbol of ultimate teenage prestige. I had already made my choice and negotiated the deal with the brother of a friend. The day I viewed it, I knew fulfillment was just around the corner. The sun glinted off its beautiful red hood as I surveyed the curves of the chassis, its one-liter engine purring like a kitten, its tidy, polished interior looking like an auto show winner. I was soon to be the proud owner of £500 ($700) worth of Talbot Samba!

After surviving three months at the factory I had enough money to purchase the car, insure it, and get some necessary extras.

The day had come when I could realize my dream. I was just nineteen, and in a small country town in Wiltshire a teenager with a car was somebody! I polished that car until the paint faded. How I enjoyed speeding away from the scooters and bicycles! But gradually, after a couple of months, I began to experience what I thought I could never feel—a pang of disappointment and a hint of boredom. I realized something else as well: Nearly everybody else's car was bigger, better, and faster than mine. In fact, I soon came to see my car as embarrassingly dull; the truth was, it couldn't pull me out of bed. In no time at all the novelty had worn off, and I wanted to change my car for something better. Perhaps a faster car could bring me true motoring happiness. Yes, the answer was certainly a Vauxhall Cavalier, the prince of sedan satisfaction!

THE UNTREATED EPIDEMIC

"The grass is always greener on the other side" is an old saying that never seems to die; indeed, the band Travis recently released a song with those very words in its lyrics. Somehow the sun is always shining somewhere else. It seems true happiness is always around the next corner, just out of our grasp over the brow of the next hill, to be found in the next job, the next relationship, the new house, or the next experience. We seek "perpetual novelty" to punctuate the dreariness of a life that can so easily become devoid of expectation, excitement, and wonder.

The story of my motoring madness didn't end with my next car, of course, nor with the one after that. Like new clothes that become familiar in the wearing, every car I've ever owned has lost its novelty before the oil needed a change. This seems to be a law of life, no matter how great our resources are to indulge our cravings. Material dissatisfaction is the great virus of the Western world. I find it remarkable, from my own experience in the developing world, that the "have nots" often exhibit a far greater degree of satisfaction in life than the "have so much they don't know what to do with it" people of the West. Like the millionaire who, when asked, "How much do you need to be happy?" replied, "Just a little bit more," we seem repeatedly disappointed that lasting satisfaction and contentment have evaded us for another year. As the Christian thinker Ravi Zacharias writes, "The loneliest moment in life is when you have just experienced what you thought would deliver the ultimate, and it has let you down."[1]

But what is the source of this persistent gnawing that refuses to give the heart rest? Why, despite all we have, do so many people find themselves miserable? The cliché that tells us "money can't buy happiness" is not swallowed by the majority of us. Wealth entices most when dangled before those still unaware of its deceitful promises.

We yearn, above all else, to be happy. We long for something more than we have, in the belief that when we have a certain experience, our longing for this vague something will be satisfied. Perhaps now the cry "There must be something more!" will finally be silenced and leave us in peace. Alas, the lion refuses to close its mouth. The predator seems insatiable, and we are caught in its jaws of misery.

There is something about the experience of being alive in this world that is, inexplicably, an encounter with anxiety, boredom, and sadness. Those who have never felt it are either too young and naive to see the pattern, or in an attempt to escape it have become dishonest with themselves. A revealing article entitled "Great House, Great Family, Great Car . . . Still Feel Miserable?" puts the weight of recent research behind this condition:

> David, 39, has just bought a new house—3,100 square feet of immaculate living space set on an acre of land in the Oxfordshire countryside. He has a pretty young wife with long, brown hair, and the money she makes as a sales manager pushes their annual income close to six figures. They travel a lot together; their last three holidays were to Hong Kong, Hawaii and the Cayman Islands. David has two young sons, aged seven and two, who consider Dad to be their hero. There's a full time nanny to take care of them when he and his wife aren't around. And although David often works long hours, it's for no one but himself. As the owner of a distributing business he's his own boss. Yes David has it all. Yet in his bedroom, locked in a dressing table drawer, is a full bottle of sleeping pills that he can't seem to chase from his thoughts. Although he's never taken them, he admits that he has considered it—more than once. So David can't help asking himself one question: Why aren't I happy? "From the outside looking in my life is great," he says. "Yet I'm not happy. I never am. And I can't understand why."[2]

I was watching a TV entertainer, Parkinson, one evening, and as usual he had some interesting guests—the comedian Billy Connolly and the singer/musician Sting. I listened with interest as Sting talked about his life and music, and something he said grabbed my attention. When asked about his wealth and success he said, "I thought success and happiness were the same thing, but when I was at my most successful, I was most unhappy."[3] This baffling unhappiness is not just true of ordinary people, then, like David; it is equally true at the top level of human achievement.

The unhappiness epidemic is being called "covert depression," symptomized by such apathy about life that people are unable to get out of bed to face another meaningless day. Working, exercising, spending, and drinking are typically used to mask a deep-seated unease. Many psychological theories exist for beating the problem, but do they reach the heart of it? Psychology professor David Lykken suggests that the human race is, "by nature, a happy breed." But is this true? Do our lives match the professor's optimistic outlook? Does world history back his statement up? Blaise Pascal is less positive: "Man's condition: inconstancy boredom anxiety."[4]

Is all this an effort to depress us further? No, it is to help us consider the true cause of our malady. The immediate source of human anxiety is our deep lack of contentment that refuses to budge, no matter how "well" we do in life—an indescribable longing for something beyond, something higher and greater than everyday life affords. But if this longing causes our agitation, where does it come from, and can it be satisfied?

LIFELONG LONGING

Although difficult to put into words, to be human is to long for something more, something beyond us. Fulfillment, peace, and lasting happiness, for no apparent reason, seem to have evaded us. We believe that we are meant for happiness and made for joy. Pain and suffering are somehow a mistake that should not be part of life.

The question remains, why do we long for anything? In the biological sense, our longings or deep-seated desires point us to an essential source of fulfillment. When thirsty, longing for a drink, we can turn on the tap for a glass of water or pop into the store for a can of Coke. After satisfying ourselves with liquid refreshment our thirst is quenched! The same can be said with regard to food, shelter, warmth, and so on. All of these natural longings can be met in the material world for those with the resources and human relationships to meet them. However, the deeper longing seems to evade satisfaction in any material way; the lingering desire for a vague something remains.

There are times, perhaps in a moment of passion and romance or in a place of great natural beauty, that we imagine the longing has been met, but the elation does not last. As C. S. Lewis puts it, "The supposed satisfaction to our deepest longing just fades away . . . something has evaded us."[5]

Yet this longing is real. It is the unseen and often unexpressed force behind much of our behavior. Deep down we believe that, like all other longings, there must be a potential source of satisfaction. "Somewhere over the rainbow," as the song puts it, or beyond the horizon or around the next bend, is an encounter that will not be a mirage, but a genuine oasis of contentment. In fact, it can be argued convincingly that the search for fulfillment is the fundamental reason for all the questing, in all its forms, of the human race. Discovery and exploration, the driving force behind the great civilizations, gained momentum primarily through the latent power of longing. It is therefore surprising that our educational system has, on the whole, sought to silence the inner voice and has attempted instead to indoctrinate us with materialist assumptions about ourselves. Yet as the philosophical and cultural climate has changed dramatically during the latter part of the last century, the voice of longing has grown louder, rejecting the claims of some of the scientific establishment.

So why should such a longing arise? This is a challenging question, because human longing seems to naturally fall into only two rational categories. First, as we have said, there is the desire to satisfy a particular natural or emotional need. Such needs are innately part of who and what we are as human beings. We have all experienced this first category; we have all been hungry and longed for a good meal. Second, it is the desire to repeat a memorable experience. I love camping in the Lake District. On a warm evening as the sun goes down, to sit, reading a good book, drinking hot chocolate, is an experience I love to repeat. We have all had experiences we long to renew. But if we hold to a worldview that excludes God, this spiritual longing and nagging dissatisfaction doesn't fit either category. There is no reasonable evolutionary reason for such a longing to arise, as it could serve no purpose in such a scheme. It is certainly not a biological function designed for the propagation of the human race, for when consistently unmet, the despair can for some reach a suicidal level. Neither does it reside in our previous experience, because that experience has evidently never been able to satisfy in any lasting way.

What then can be the root cause of this dissatisfaction? Pascal, again with penetrating clarity of insight, writes, "Human beings do not know their place and purpose. They have fallen from their true place, and lost their true purpose. They search everywhere for their place and purpose, with great anxiety. But they cannot find them because they are surrounded by darkness."[6] Our place and our purpose in this world are at the very root of the great yearnings and longings we experience. We are told there must be some highly technical psychological or genetic explanation for all this, but the truth seems much simpler. Instinctively we expect our longings to be met outside ourselves—our desires and emotions push us outward. New Age gurus, and even popular songwriters, tell us to withdraw into ourselves and peer into our own souls for happiness—but this fails to solve the longing.

The picture becomes clearer when we read the words of Solomon (the Preacher) in the Bible: "[God] has planted eternity in the human heart, but even so, people cannot see the whole scope of God's work from beginning to end" (Ecclesiastes 3:11, NLT).

According to Solomon, our longing becomes a signpost to the only source of satisfaction; our spiritual longing—this sense of eternity—has been planted there by God himself and is part of our human makeup. Our yearning is also an echo of Eden, an inescapable reminder of a time in human history when the longing was satisfied, when human experience was bliss, and the soul found joy and contentment in relationship with its Creator. It is, to put it another way, a latent memory of an experience that we long to renew, that of knowing God himself.

THREE SIDES OF THE STORY

The most often visited Internet site of summer 2001 was reported to be that offering an interview with God. A London newspaper stated that www.reata.org was "attracting millions of surfers." Written by an American Sunday school teacher, the website offers an imaginary question-and-answer session with God. One question was, "What surprises you most about humankind?" The answer was, "That they get bored with childhood. They rush to grow up and then long to be children again. That they lose their health to make money and then lose their money to restore their health." The online measuring agency Jupiter Media Metrix counted an amazing 2.4 million visitors in June alone. The site claimed that six million people around the world had logged on since the end of May 2001, and all this without advertising!

It seems we are still longing for a divine conversation to answer our cry. We are still looking for answers to the basic questions about life and human nature. We are still seeking the other side of the story. We are not merely biochemical machines composed of billions of atoms. There is more to us than the sum of our parts, and we are not just advanced mammals that happen to walk on two legs. We are aware of three sides to our conscious nature. We are obviously physical beings, with appetites that are met by the physical world, and those appetites demand satisfaction from this source only. These desires develop early and end at death.

The second side to our nature is the intellect. We are intelligent beings, capable of knowledge, and have a strong desire to know things. We have an aptitude for inquiry and long to know "why." I was just old enough to find comical my youngest brother's constant questioning about anything and everything. He would not let us rest until he had an answer. When he asked me a question such as "How fast can a rhino run?" I would bluff that I knew the answer, just to shut him up. It is this questioning that sets us apart from the likes of the rhino. Almost as soon as a baby can focus his or her eyes, he or she gazes at his or her mother as if to ask a thousand questions, before he or she can ever speak a word. We don't find that with a cat or a budgie. The kitten plays with its siblings and is fascinated by its surroundings, but provide for its basic needs and the household pet is satisfied. My dog, Samson, lies at my feet and does not ask any questions. He has never turned to me to ask "Who am I?" or "Why am I here?" He is satisfied with warmth, contact, and food. The capacity for abstract thought is simply not present. However, the infant is a natural philosopher. Intellectual appetite resides in our nature as powerfully as the appetite for life itself and demands satisfaction. The whole universe is open for us to feed our inquiring minds. Throughout recorded history we have always asked the big questions and sought answers. The very stance and frame of human beings and the placement of our eyes is one that looks up and out, not snuffling in the ground. You are reading this book because you are seeking explanations to the reason for certain things and wish to inquire about them.

Physical appetites assume a source of fulfillment; so does our appetite for knowledge and truth. Ironically, those who state that there is no "true" reason of things essentially contradict themselves by asserting that "the reason of things is that there is no reason of things." All logically sound philosophical inquiry proves what I am saying; truth is inescapable, and to deny this is itself an appeal to the truth. We demand to know what is true and cannot defeat this urge. The pursuit of science, philosophy, and culture is the story of that urge's outworking.

This chapter has really been about the third side of our nature. We are physical beings, we are intelligent beings, but we are also spiritual and moral beings. No matter how hard we try to escape this reality, human beings have an irresistible longing that is correlated to God. This is expressed not only in an innate desire to worship, but in the need to understand what life is about—how we are to live and what we are to live for. In short, what the meaning and purpose of life is and how we can be happy. We therefore raise questions about right and wrong. We find ourselves troubled and uneasy inside because of our behavior and that of others. Sometimes a strange guilt oppresses us, but we cannot easily identify the cause. We have a sense of ultimate accountability for our actions, even when we consider ourselves answerable to no one. These feelings can be summed up in the word *conscience*, a self-knowledge about good and bad, right and wrong, an internal policeman whom we either ignore or heed. The Bible teaches that God has put this "law" in the heart and that only through obedience to the voice of conscience can we begin to address the spiritual longings of the moral side of our nature.

Keeping these things we know about ourselves in mind, I would argue that we no more need proof of God than a baby needs proof that food is available or that a child needs proof of things to be known. The existence of God, a recognition of accountability, and a sense of moral duty are all assumed as readily as the other categories of appetite. We may seek to escape this or reason it away (and some people resent the implications), but it lingers still. The fact that some people will go to great lengths to oppose the demands of their own conscience and the claims of God simply demonstrates this. People who identify them-selves as "atheists in a meaningless world" do so on the basis of a moral decision to live in contradiction to their conscience, and not because of intellectual certitude. Aldous Huxley willingly admitted:

> I had motives for not wanting the world to have a meaning; con-sequently I assumed it had none, and was able, without any dif-ficulty, to find satisfying reasons for this assumption. Most ignorance is invincible ignorance. We don't know because we don't want to know. The philosopher who finds no meaning in the world is not concerned exclusively with a problem in pure metaphysics; he is also concerned to prove that there is no valid reason why he personally should not do as he wants to do, or why his friends should not seize political power and govern in a way they find most advantageous to themselves. . . . For myself, as, no doubt, for most of my contemporaries, the phi-losophy of meaninglessness was essentially an instrument of my liberation.[7]

He goes on to point out that the liberation to which he refers is eco-nomic, political, and sexual. Hence we find that most of our assump-tions are morally driven.

The teaching of the Bible and the Christian faith in dealing with this notion is clear: You cannot find peace and happiness this way; you can try, but you will fail. This sort of liberation is not freedom at all. To live life by the code of "do as you please regardless" is to become a prisoner of your own moral corruption. It is to be troubled by guilt and tormented by the inconsistency of living contrary to the demands of your own conscience and moral nature. You simply cannot be sat-isfied while ignoring any part of your nature. St. Augustine wrote, "You [God] have made us for yourself, and our hearts are restless until they find their rest in you."[8]

The teaching of Jesus in the Bible tackles our struggle head-on. Jesus taught that the demand of our heart (moral nature) for virtue holds the secret of happiness. He taught that without purity and moral rightness, which the Bible calls holiness, we can never be happy or find fulfillment. He explained that the route to this moral rightness was through a relationship with God and obedience to him: "Blessed are those who hunger and thirst for righteousness, for they shall be satisfied. . . . Blessed are the pure in heart, for they shall see God" (Matthew 5:6, 8, NASB). Or, to paraphrase it in modern English, "Happy are those who long and yearn for moral rightness, for they will be satisfied. . . . Happy are the pure in heart, for they will know God" (my version).

Jesus taught that in God is all lasting joy, happiness, and contentment! It is in living in accordance with the character of God, by his moral law, expressed in our own conscience and his commandments, that happiness is pursued and found. We experience the power and reality of this in the smallest of ways—when we encourage or forgive someone, when we selflessly give gifts, when we give back the extra change to the cashier, when we are able to lift someone's spirits. We are all familiar with the opposite effect of regret—when we speak unfairly to a loved one, when we are abusive to a stranger, when we gossip about another person, when we are selfish with our possessions. In those reflective moments of the day, there are numerous events or circumstances we may regret because of our actions.

The truth is, if we trace the problems of our own existence, at every turn our Creator confronts us. We cannot find ourselves without finding God. When we see ourselves clearly, we see that nothing and no one but God can supply our spiritual and moral needs. The more we try, the less we can make ourselves happy without God. Pascal writes about the frustration:

> We desire the truth, but find within ourselves nothing but uncertainty. We seek happiness, but find mainly misery. We are incapable of suppressing the desire for truth and happiness, and yet are incapable of knowing truth and happiness. These frustrated desires remind us how far we have fallen from our true state.[9]

SOUL STARVATION

If we do not meet the demands of our physical nature for food, we become sick and finally die. If we ignore our intellect, depriving the mental side of our nature of all learning, imagination, exploration, questioning, and discovery, we drive ourselves to despair and, ultimately, madness. And it is equally true that if we neglect and ignore the moral and spiritual side of our nature, we become morally and spiritually sick, and moral and spiritual death ensues. The symptoms of the sickness are those I have been describing. The mystery illness of "covert depression" is a moral and spiritual disease.

As surely as the stomach rumbles for food and the mind questions after truth, so the soul longs for God and for virtue. Our yearnings are our appetite for God. If we fail to recognize this, unhappiness and a sense of something missing will give way to overwhelming guilt, fear, despair, and moral confusion. These feelings either grow in intensity or disappear altogether, leaving us feeling empty, without any desire for God or moral truth, like a starving stomach unable to hold down food.

It is a big shock to many when these problems first surface—perhaps in our late twenties or early thirties. We satisfy our bodies and minds from the very beginning but often ignore our moral and spiritual nature, and then wonder why we have such a void within, despite having the material things we thought we always wanted. We live in a culture that is morally adrift, desperately searching for meaning and absolutes to anchor the soul.

Jesus Christ is the only remedy for this condition: The Bible presents a feast for the soul in the person of Christ. Jesus claimed, "I am the bread of life. No one who comes to me will ever be hungry again. Those who believe in me will never thirst" (John 6:35, NLT). He said this shortly after his miracle of feeding five thousand men plus women and children (about fifteen to twenty thousand people in total) with five loaves of bread and two fish—a small boy's packed lunch. Jesus had fed the hungry people physically, but he knew that this was not the root of the human problem. A fish sandwich cannot nourish the human heart. In the remarkable statement recorded in John 6:35, Jesus says that just as the life of the body is nourished by food, so true spiritual life is found in him. He is not saying, "Come to me and you will never have to go to the market again." His theme is not fruit and vegetables. He is calling people to himself, the true source of food for the soul, where the longings of the human heart are met. Bread and water feed the temporary life of the body. But he offers himself as true, eternal, spiritual bread for all who hunger and thirst for God and for righteousness.

In a world suffering from soul starvation, the words of Jesus not only strike us as unique and powerful, but as pregnant with great comfort and hope. Our society promises much but delivers little; so we become disillusioned. But if we will abandon our illusions and the vanity of so many of our pursuits for just the briefest of moments, we may hear the voice of Christ whispering to us what he said to longing, searching people two thousand years ago: "My purpose is to give life in all its fullness" (John 10:10, NLT).

We shall in a later chapter examine the claims and promises of Jesus Christ more fully. I have mentioned some of his words here because they highlight for us a need in our lives that goes beyond the material world and its pursuits, to God himself, the only hope of a lasting cure for the sickness of the soul.

CLOSED EYES SEE NOTHING

So far in this book I have stressed the importance of carefully considering our worldview and asking the important questions concerning what we believe and why we believe it. We have seen that questions of meaning, purpose, and truth are at the very heart of what it means to be human. We have looked at reasons to believe that God is both real and relevant to our lives and have examined several popular fallacies concerning origins that would try to silence any discussion about these things before we start. In this chapter we have identified the great desires common to us all in different ways, and I have gone on to infer that this points us to God as the sole answer to our longings.

Yet I do not pretend to have shown you God clearly, as such a claim would be dishonest. Indeed, the Bible itself declares, "No one has ever seen God" (1 John 4:12, NLT). The Bible teaches that to a certain degree God has hidden himself, and that human beings are surrounded by the darkness of ignorance. But the Bible does present us with two facts that I have sought to establish.

First, God has left many signs of himself, both within and outside us, that can be recognized by those who are seeking him (Romans 1:19-20). And second, these signs are camouflaged in the human experience in such a way that those who do not seek him will neither see nor understand them (John 1:10-13). If we do not seek, we cannot see, we will not see. But Jesus taught that if we seek, we will find—if we seek with all our hearts! Therefore, the only way to succeed in our search is to follow the injunction of the Bible that "Anyone who wants to come to him must believe that there is a God and that he rewards those who sincerely seek him" (Hebrews 11:6, NLT).

6

Bible Bashers

How petty are the books of the philosophers with all their pomp compared with the gospels.

JEAN-JACQUES ROUSSEAU

There is no book upon which we can rest in a dying moment, but the Bible.

JOHN SELDEN

FOOD FOR THE SOUL

One terrifying day Howard Rutledge's plane was shot down over Vietnam. He managed to parachute out but landed in a village where he was beaten, stripped, and thrown into prison. Thus began a brutal incarceration, lasting seven years, that can only be described as a living hell: eating rotting soup and animal fat, in the company of spiders the size of a human hand and rats the size of cats. He was cold, alone, and tortured, left in pools of his own waste, chained in agonizing positions and being eaten alive by insects feasting on his open sores. He later wrote a book of his experiences called *In the Presence of Mine Enemies*, where he describes those years and how he stayed sane through the horror. He writes:

Now the sights and sounds and smells of death were all around me. My hunger for spiritual food soon outdid my hunger for a steak. Now I wanted to know about that part of me that will never die. Now I wanted to talk about God and Christ and the church. But in Heartbreak [the name they gave to their prison] solitary confinement there was no pastor, no Sunday-school teacher, no Bible, no hymnbook, no community of believers to guide and sustain me. I had completely neglected the spiritual dimension of my life. It took prison to show me how empty life is without God, and so I had to go back in my memory to those Sunday-school days in Tulsa, Oklahoma. If I couldn't have a Bible and hymn book, I would try to rebuild them in my mind. . . . Most of my fellow prisoners were struggling like me to rediscover faith, to reconstruct workable value systems. . . . Everyone knew the Lord's prayer and the Twenty-third Psalm, but the camp favorite verse that everyone recalled first and quoted most often is found in the Gospel of John, third chapter, sixteenth verse ["for God so loved the world that he gave his only Son, that everyone who believes in him may not perish but may have eternal life," NRSV] . . . how I struggled to recall those scriptures and hymns. . . . Remember, we weren't playing games. The enemy knew that the best way to break a man's resistance was to crush his spirit in a lonely cell. In other words, some of our POWs after solitary confinement lay down in a fetal position and died. All this talk of scripture and hymns may seem boring to some, but it was the way we conquered our enemy and overcame the power of death around us.[1]

The Bible is not just another book. It stands out above Shakespeare, Milton, Dickens, or other religious writings. These soldiers were not trying to recall nursery rhymes or even Tolstoy and Blake; instead, they desperately tried to remember the words of the Bible.

Something has kept this book, to this day, at the top of the best-seller list every year. What is it that makes it so special? The word *Bible* literally means "the book." Whatever we may at present believe or think about the Bible, the influence for good that it has exerted upon the globe is immeasurable.

TIMELESS INSPIRATION

The basic principles of our legal system (British New World and North American) come directly from the teaching of the Bible. The Ten Commandments hang on the walls of England's courts. The freedom we enjoy in our society today is the result of the teaching of the Bible when correctly applied. Lord Denning, a leading civil lawyer in the 1960s and 1970s, claimed that our civil law had been molded by judges brought up believing the Bible. He concluded, "If religion perishes in the land, truth and justice will also."[2]

The impact of biblical Christianity on modern science has also been far-reaching. Robert Boyle, Michael Faraday, Lord Kelvin (a founder of modern physics), James Maxwell, and Sir Ambrose Fleming are all legendary names in science, and all are members of the Royal Society. They believed the Bible's message, claiming it was central to their work. Great medical practitioners have been deeply committed to and inspired by the Bible, including Sir Joseph Lister (antiseptic surgery), Sir James Simpson (discovered anesthetic), and Arthur Rendle Short (pioneered blood transfusions). Again, it was the message of the Bible that inspired the first hospitals. For hundreds of years the church provided almost the only care for the sick and dying. Christians funded the first hospitals, among them London's St Bartholomew's in 1123 and Guy's in 1741.

Modern education too was largely the creation of the Christian church. After the Reformation in the sixteenth century, numerous schools were founded. In England and Scotland every parish provided a school and schoolmaster. Millions were educated in this way, long before state education began [in England] in 1870. The distribution of the Bible was crucial in bringing literacy to common people from the time of the reformer William Tyndale. In North America great institutions like Yale and Princeton began as Christian colleges to prepare people to be ministers.

The influence the Bible has had on the arts is also striking. One need only glance at Milton, Blake, Shakespeare, Brontë, or Austen to see this, and the biblically inspired music of J. S. Bach, Handel, and Mendelssohn is arguably some of the most beautiful ever composed.

England at the beginning of the eighteenth century had neglected the Bible and had become a cruel, violent place. But when two Christian preachers, John Wesley and George Whitefield, took to the streets and fields to preach about Jesus Christ, things began to change dramatically. Many historians believe that this revival of Christianity saved England from a bloody revolution like that in France. Prison reform began to take place through John Howard, and through the dedication of William Wilberforce (a committed Christian) the slave trade was abolished in 1833. Wilberforce's Christian friends, the Clapham Sect, established and financed the colony of Sierra Leone as a home for freed slaves and gave its capital the name Freetown. Other Christians inspired by the Scriptures, like James Tolpuddle, pioneered the trade unions in England to improve the working conditions of ordinary men and women. Lord Shaftesbury is a famous social reformer who campaigned for clean water, proper sanitation, and an end to child labor. He supported orphanages and worked to improve conditions for women and the mentally ill. He openly admitted that his views were due to his allegiance to Jesus Christ and the teaching of the Bible. At his funeral in 1885 the streets were lined with people he had labored to help, who carried banners with words from Matthew 25:35. In the *New Living Translation* this reads: "I was a stranger, and you invited me into your home."

All of this is just the tip of the iceberg. By the late nineteenth century three quarters of all charitable organizations were run by Christians. In England Barnardos, the NSPCC, Oxfam, Christian Aid, the Leprosy Mission, and Elizabeth Fry's women's prison reform are just a few of the many charities that were sparked by the revival of Christianity and the teaching of the Bible that took place in the eighteenth century. Similar things could be said about New England in the early nineteenth century through the likes of Charles Finney and many others. None of these is faultless or ever claimed to be so, but they left on record the source of their motivation. The Bible has changed society, not as a plethora of rules, but because its message changes people. After all, society is a collection of individuals learning to live together. Change the individual and you can change the world.

JUST LOOKING

Sadly, when looking at this remarkable book, the Bible, many people approach it in a purely theoretical way, considering it to be just another interesting topic of conversation, like music or fashion. Discussions about the Bible are often described as "simply for people who like that sort of thing" or of intellectual interest "if that takes one's fancy." But the Bible does not come across as a piece of literature merely to be studied and analyzed. The POWs in Vietnam were not trying to recall Bible verses for their literary beauty or to play deconstructionist games; they were seeking to draw on the Bible's power to feed their souls in a time of desperation.

While the Bible does contain important history, politics, poetry, and philosophy that are of great benefit to study, it is much more than that. It is a book about the human race, about us! It addresses our problems, both global and personal. Tackling the human tragedy, the Bible tells us how to be rescued from the loneliness, guilt, and sadness of life and empowers us to change for the better. But perhaps most astonishingly of all, it challenges each person to test its claims in his or her own life. It does not simply claim to be true but invites rigorous examination and promises to demonstrate its truthfulness when its message is put to the test.

FACTUAL FOUNDATIONS

The Bible is unique in many ways. Unlike all other religions (Judaism excepted), Christianity is based upon historical acts and facts. All other faiths center on the subjective ethical teaching of their founders, but the Christian faith is built upon the great events of Bible history— Creation, the Fall, the Flood, the giving of the Ten Commandments, the virgin birth, the crucifixion, and the resurrection. They involve real people in real events. It is not a collection of disjointed and mystical stories or the collected teachings of a prophet or sage. Although the teaching of Jesus is very important, Christianity does not hang on his teaching alone but upon who he was and what he did. Few familiar with the Bible would doubt that Jesus is the greatest teacher who ever lived, but Jesus taught that who he is is just as important.

Consequently, the Bible is not a book of elevated moral philosophy or eloquent prose but is based on objective, historical facts open to verification. The Bible does not ask us to accept an ethical teaching simply because it says so. Instead, it calls on us to test its coherence and validity. The Bible is an account of what God has done for us in human history and how he has spoken and acted in our world, which is why we can test the Bible to see whether it is true. All other religious texts fail the same tests—the Bible alone stands as a beacon of truth, as we shall see.

OBJECTION SUSTAINED?

So, can biblical claims be trusted and substantiated? Is there internal or external evidence for them? We shall see that indeed there is a great deal of evidence to support the Bible's claims. Compare the Bible to another religious text such as the Qur'an, for example. Muslims claim that the Qur'an is a revelation from God to Muhammad. The only evidence offered in defense of this claim is the existence of the Qur'an itself—a circular argument! There are no miracles and no credible witnesses to substantiate Muhammad's claims recorded in the Qur'an, and crucially no resurrection. Indeed, Muhammad denied that he did any miracles except for the writing of the Qur'an. Later the Hadith (Muslim traditions of the words and deeds of Muhammad) starts attributing various miracles to him. For instance, the Meccans asked Muhammad to do a miracle to prove he was Allah's prophet. He supposedly reached up with his sword and cut the moon in half![3]

Furthermore, the Qur'an makes numerous historical, geographical, and factual errors. For example, it describes biblical characters as diverse as Mary the mother of Jesus, Moses, and Abraham all living and working together, whereas they lived hundreds of years apart! It is claimed that Alexander the Great (Zul-qarnain) was a Muslim who lived to an old age (Sura 18:89-98). But history shows that he was neither a Muslim, nor did he live a long life. (The *Encyclopaedia Britannica* explains that Muhammad's account is derived from a romance about Alexander from the seventh century A.D.) The Qur'an further claims that Alexander the Great followed the setting of the sun, which went down into the waters of a muddy spring (Sura 18:85-86).

People must make up their own minds about whether they wish to base their lives on fables or follow the teachings of a book rooted in real history.

Many facets come into play when testing the Bible's reliability and its claim to have been inspired by God. Does it describe the human condition accurately? Is its history backed by archaeology and other historical sources? Have any of its prophecies been fulfilled? Does it follow a logical thread and coherent structure over the thousands of years in which it was written? Are the accounts from genuine eyewitnesses? How reliable are the manuscript copies? When were the Gospels written, and by whom? Does the Bible change people's lives for the better? These and many other questions can be answered satisfactorily and in the affirmative as we look at the Scriptures. The Bible has proven itself, in the face of ceaseless onslaught, especially since the higher schools of thought in the nineteenth century, to be reliable in the details its authors record.

It is vital to remember that if someone objects to the biblical account, they must demonstrate either the unreliability and incompetence of an author or historically falsify the record or claim.

THE GOD WHO SPEAKS

In a previous chapter we evaluated the rational conclusion that God created the universe, fashioning with great purpose and skill the world in which we live, with all its intricacy, beauty, and wonder. This is a form of revelation from God: He speaks in an important sense through his creation! If there is a God who created this world, then just as a painting reveals the imagination and mind of the artist, so the creation reveals something of the character and nature of God—not only through the stars, animals, and majestic beauty of the natural world, but also through the existence of a moral law within us and the unique wonder of human consciousness.

From ancient times the greatest names in philosophy—Plato, Aristotle, and Socrates—have affirmed the existence of a divine being, but have admitted to being largely in the dark as to what form he takes or what his requirements are. For example, one recurring question in theology and philosophy has been, can God forgive wrongdoing?

If God made this universe and communicates certain things about his nature through the natural world and our conscience, it is conceivable that he could give further revelation about his character, will, and relationship to us. If, as our conscience teaches us, love and justice are desirable virtues, then these reflect the attributes of our Creator. Such a God would surely not leave us in the dark about who he is, who we are, and how we are to relate. It would be strange indeed if God were to create and abandon, in silence, his creation, leaving no indicators but those of our existence and the tangible world. Who would have children, place them in the home, and never speak to them again?

A silent, loving God does not meet our expectations, and so sounds more like a contradiction in terms. We feel a sense of accountability for our actions, but to understand this we need further revelation (understanding) of the nature and outworking of that accountability. We carry a sense of guilt for doing wrong; so we need further revelation to understand whether this can be forgiven. We assume our own immortality; thus we need further revelation to understand where we go after death, and who we will face when we depart on that final journey. We see all around us the tragedy of evil, pain, and suffering, but we need further revelation to understand how the world came to be as it is and whether it can be changed. Thus revelation from God is not only possible but necessary, if he is good and just. In other words, it is reasonable to expect God to speak and make himself known more fully.

THE BIBLE ON THE BIBLE

Christians believe that the Bible is the revelation of a loving Creator God. The Christian faith rests squarely on the authority and authenticity of this book. It answers the ultimate questions that we have with regard to our lives and relationship to our Creator. A good starting place, then, is to ask what the Bible says about itself. Simply, there are four key passages that show what biblical authors said about the Scriptures.

In 2 Timothy 3:16-17 (NLT) the apostle Paul makes it clear that:

All Scripture is inspired by God and is useful to teach us what is true and to make us realize what is wrong in our lives. It straight-

ens us out and teaches us to do what is right. It is God's way of
preparing us in every way, fully equipped for every good thing God
want us to do.

The original Greek language here implies that all the written documents of Scripture are from God and inspired by him. Paul is referring
to the Old Testament documents that were part of the canon of
Scripture and to New Testament documents that were already in circulation. He was not referring to oral traditions or contemporary ideas.

In 2 Peter 1:20-21 (NRSV) the apostle Peter also points to the origin of the Scriptures. He states, "No prophecy ever came by human
will, but men and women moved by the Holy Spirit spoke from God."
Peter is explaining the divine origin of Scripture but also shows that
it was given through people whom God chose to use. As they wrote,
they were carried along by God so that the message was not theirs but
God's. The things they wrote were not of their own invention but were
given to them by God. When we consider that God is the Creator and
sustainer of the universe, it is not difficult to believe that he could
direct human authors in what they should say. If he did not use human
authors, how could we possibly comprehend a divine message?

In another crucial passage, 1 Timothy 5:18, Paul quotes from two
Bible passages—the fifth book of the Old Testament (Deuteronomy
25:4) and Jesus' words in the Gospel of Luke (10:7). This is important
for several reasons. First, it shows that Paul gave equal authority to the
Old and New Testaments (even though the latter was not yet complete), affirming that they are both from God. Second, it shows that
from the earliest time (that of Jesus' disciples), the Gospels were
referred to as "scripture" and continued to be considered so by the early
church. The church did not evolve the idea of the authority of the Bible
or later develop the idea of inspiration. These were taken for granted.

Finally, in 2 Peter 3:16 Peter refers to the writings of Paul as
"scripture." This is important, because in doing so he puts the words
of Paul on a par with those of Moses, King David, and Jesus himself.
As Paul is responsible for a large portion of the New Testament, this
is a significant pronouncement from Peter.

Many more statements in the Bible affirm its claim to divine inspiration. These claims cannot be taken lightly nor dismissed easily. Because of the Bible's view of itself, ultimately we have just two choices: Either the ancient Jews and early disciples are telling the truth, or they are fabricators of a heinous deception involving centuries of collaboration. To say that the Bible is a great book of holy teaching, but not inspired (given) by God, is nonsensical. Both cannot be true. It is either what it claims to be or it is false, unworthy of honest people's attention. In order to refute the Bible's witness about itself, the prosecution needs evidence. One would need to produce material evidence to show that it cannot be true, such as definitive archeological or textual evidence that refutes biblical claims. One would also need a host of circumstantial evidence to provide a reasonable motive for the deception. Indeed, the prosecution would need to show beyond reasonable doubt that the witness of the Bible is false.

JESUS ON THE BIBLE

Jesus himself repeatedly affirmed the absolute authority and divine origin of the Scriptures. This is important because it relates to the character and trustworthiness of Christ himself. Jesus constantly referred to, appealed to, and affirmed the Hebrew Scriptures of his day—the same thirty-nine books of our Old Testament. He rejected the additional traditions of religious leaders, as well as the Apocrypha (books that were excluded from the final canon), as being part of Scripture. He clearly taught that the Scriptures originated with God and were not the result of human ingenuity, and he often called them the "Word of God."

Jesus also accepted the history taught in the Bible as factual and therefore accurate, including the miraculous occurrences it records. This includes his references to the creation of men and women, a worldwide devastating flood at the time of Noah, Moses and the giving of the Ten Commandments, the burning bush, and the ministry of the prophet Elijah (see Matthew 15:3-6; 19:4; 24:37-39; Mark 12:26; Luke 4:25). Clearly, Jesus affirmed the inspiration, authority, and dependability of the Bible in all its historic contents.

In the Gospel of John (10:34-38) Jesus makes a direct claim to being God and in so doing says that the Scriptures cannot be broken.

To justify his claim he quotes from Psalm 82:6. Thus the Scriptures stand or fall with the person of Christ, because he not only affirmed their validity but claimed that they testified about him, showing that he was indeed the Son of God. We cannot separate the issue of the Bible's truth from the truthfulness of Christ. We are faced with a further choice: Either Jesus spoke the truth, in which case the Bible is revelation from God, or Jesus is a liar (or perhaps deluded, misled, or mad) and the Bible is not from God. There is no third option.

Genuine Christianity embraces the Bible as the truth, which is one of the reasons why reading the Bible is so important to a Christian. This now includes the New Testament, which Jesus promised would come into existence, inspired by God and given through his disciples (see John 14:26; 15:26-27). What the Bible says about itself and what Jesus said about it are together the starting place for understanding its importance and considering its reliability.

OUT OF THIS WORLD

It has been said, "Give me a candle and a Bible and shut me up in a dark dungeon, and I will tell you what the whole world is doing."[4] There seems to be an uncanny ring of truth about the Bible, a transcultural relevance unaffected by the passing centuries. This has led many to make astonishing statements about it. Abraham Lincoln, the sixteenth president of the United States, claimed, "All things desirable to men are contained in the Bible."[5]

Robert Dick Wilson, one of the greatest scholars of our time, writes, "I have come to the conclusion that no man knows enough to assail the truthfulness of the Old Testament."[6]

What can account for a book like this? If we deny both Jesus' and the Bible's testimony about itself, we need valid reasons for doing so; in fact, we need another tenable explanation for its existence, which proves problematic! How can one explain the origin of the Bible and its teaching if it is not from God? The early English reformer and preacher Thomas Watson was taken up with this issue when he wrote:

> I wonder whence the scripture should come if not from God. Bad men could not be the authors of it. Would their minds be

employed in dictating such holy lines? Would they declare so
freely against sin? Could good men be the authors of it? Could
they write in such a strain? Or could it stand with their grace to
counterfeit God's name and put 'thus saith the Lord' to a book
of their own devising?[7]

Watson was highlighting a spiritual problem: It is difficult to believe
that either good or bad persons were the authors of the Bible. Would
good people lie? Could evil people come up with the words of Christ?
This considered, is not the most likely explanation that it came from
God, who inspired the human authors? Even those known at times for
their dislike of Christianity have been perplexed by the very existence
of the Bible. Jean-Jacques Rousseau commented:

> I must confess to you that the majesty of the scriptures aston-
> ishes me; the holiness of the evangelists speaks to my heart and
> has such striking characters of truth, and is, moreover, so per-
> fectly inimitable, that if it had been the invention of men, the
> inventors would be greater than the greatest heroes.[8]

Charles Dickens described the Bible as "the very best book that ever
was or ever will be known in the world."[9]

Who then are these people who penned the New Testament, if not
the inspired eyewitnesses and disciples of Christ? Where did they disappear to in history? Why did they not lay claim to the greatest work
in existence? Why does history have no record of them, and why do
all the known sources point to the authorship claimed by the
Scriptures? To reject the Bible, these sorts of questions must be convincingly explained!

The Bible is remarkable even in literary terms. It has been an international bestseller for hundreds of years and is available in over two
thousand languages. It has become the most quoted, debated, and
influential book in history. But an appeal to popularity does not prove
the case. Books about Princess Diana have sold by the shipload over
the past few years with all kinds of ideas about her life and death being
presented, but we require more than sales figures to establish the reliability of the contents. Do the Scriptures hold up to truth tests?

ALLEGED CONTRADICTIONS

One of the most impressive things about the Bible is that although it contains sixty-six books by forty-four authors from peasants to kings and was composed over thousands of years, it forms a cohesive whole. The flow of history, logic, and thought is striking, and all stand or fall together. Remarkably, there is no evidence of collusion or forgery. Every author is an individual with a given style, emphasis, and historical context, often separated by centuries. It is this fact that makes its teaching so compelling. Yet for some, the accusation of contradictions in the Bible is a foregone conclusion. In my experience, those who have never actually studied the Bible for themselves often shout this the loudest. A lot of today's pop knowledge concerning the Bible is derived from talk shows, television and radio debates, throw-away comments in the restaurant or pub, or misinformed school and university teachers with prejudiced views. It is easy to state the Bible is full of contradictions, but quite another to prove it!

A logical contradiction involves asserting the truth of two opposites at the same time. To say that my jumper is red and in the same breath refer to it as blue constitutes a contradiction. But if I were to say that my father's name is Michael and he is a Dutchman at heart, while my wife insists her father-in-law's name is Boot and that he is Welsh on the surface might seem contradictory. However, when we understand the context, the apparent discrepancy is cleared up. My father's surname is Boot, and his father is Dutch, but his first name is Michael, and he was born in Wales while his dad was stationed there in the Navy.

The difference between the red jumper statements and the family origin statements is important. The first is a factual contradiction, the second a complementary difference in account. It is a contradictory claim or fact that needs to be shown to constitute a contradiction, not a complementary one.

Imagine that together with two of your work colleagues you were asked to write an account of the occurrences in the office that day. Despite being in the same room, at the same meetings, witnessing the same events, your reports would differ considerably in style, emphasis, and observational detail. You would notice and recall things that others did not, and vice versa. You might include certain facts that you considered significant that others left out. Yet if you were all seeking to report the truth, while your accounts would highlight different things, they would give a broad factual and objective picture of the day's events, expressed from several perspectives. This is precisely the role of a witness in court. In this way real history can be known, and written texts can be meaningful in an objective sense.

So when we come to look at the New Testament we must be aware of certain things. For example, the Gospel writers do not all put the activities of Jesus in precisely the same order. The writers of the time did not see the exact chronology of events as paramount. What happened was more important than precisely when. Sometimes the Bible is not aiming at absolute precision; where it has not been aimed at, it should not be expected. If a material witness says, "I was walking down the road and heard a loud scream at about 11 P.M.," he or she is not a liar if a bystander noticed that at the time of the scream the town clock read 11:03 P.M.

A surface reading of the things that at first appear to contradict in fact complement each other and do not alter the overall message. So when we examine the context of an alleged contradiction, we should check the original language, take into account the culture and history, and assess the intention of the author, and the supposed discrepancies may disappear. This is what scholarship is about. And fair-minded scholarship has consistently affirmed the Bible.

To find the objective truth and meaning, we are looking for the literal reading of the passage. This means that we believe the writer said what he intended to say, and we do not force another idea on the text! Finding this intention is the key. When King David wrote in Psalm 23:1 that "The LORD is my shepherd," he did not mean that God actually is a shepherd; this is a figure of speech to describe God's character as one who cares, guides, and provides. People often remark in dismay, "You don't take the Bible literally, do you?" This demonstrates a confused outlook. Yes, we do take the Bible literally, in that we accept what the writers intended to say. When the apostle John records Jesus' words about heaven as a real place to which he will take believers when he returns, we accept that this is what Jesus was trying to say, rather than pretending that Jesus merely meant we can create a heaven on earth and in our hearts.

Many brilliant scholars who have dedicated their lives to the study of the Bible have emerged with ever greater confidence in its trustworthiness. Gleason Archer, Professor of Old Testament and Semitic Studies, writes:

> I have dealt with one apparent discrepancy after another and have studied the alleged contradictions between the Biblical record and the evidence of linguistics, archaeology or science. My confidence in the trustworthiness of scripture has been repeatedly verified and strengthened by the discovery that almost every problem in scripture that has ever been discovered by man from ancient times until now, has been dealt with in a completely satisfactory manner by the Biblical text itself, or else by objective archaeological information.[10]

The Scriptures teach that God is all-knowing and does not contradict himself, and so Christians believe that God's Word, when rightly understood, is not contradictory. A simple study of the Bible is the best way to test this and see for ourselves the clarity and truthfulness of this Book. Supposed contradictions disappear, and we derive great benefit from coming to grips with its message. In the words of Theodore Roosevelt, "A thorough knowledge of the Bible is worth more than a college education."[11]

He Did What?

To list the miracles contained in the Bible would take a great deal of time. The Bible records numerous supernatural occurrences that defy our notion of "laws" of nature. Christianity is a supernatural belief in a supernatural God. Or to put it another way, the Bible teaches that there is much more to the universe than the material world; therefore material "laws" (uniformities) can be defied! From parting the Red Sea, feeding multitudes with a packed lunch, and restoring the sight of the blind, to the virgin birth and the resurrection, the Bible is obsolete without the supernatural. Emptied of this divine activity, it would have nothing left but a handful of platitudes.

That the Bible records many supernatural events is difficult for some skeptics, who consequently reject it without giving it a fair hearing. Some are of the opinion that miracles cannot happen; so the Bible is dismissed by default. The philosopher David Hume was largely responsible for popularizing this objection. His argument can be summarized in this way:

1. The laws of nature cannot be violated.
2. Miracles are violations of the laws of nature.
3. Therefore miracles do not occur.

The faulty basis of this reasoning is obvious—it is a circular argument. He assumes as true what he is trying to prove. He makes an assumption that can't be proved. When it comes to miraculous occurrences, the question to be asked is not, *can* it happen, but *did* it happen? Can these accounts be trusted? Scientific objections based on naturalistic, philosophical assumptions cannot be used as "evidence," because we cannot reproduce a historical situation in a laboratory in order to test it. If I claim my grandfather was bad-tempered, I cannot test that claim in a laboratory, but must gather evidence from eyewitnesses and assess my claim on the strength of their evidence. Or if I told you that some years ago my roommate in college was instantly cured of chronic deafness in one ear after being prayed for by a Christian, a scientific experiment cannot corroborate my report. You would need to interview him, his family, his friends, his workmates, and the person who prayed for him. And you could go to the Royal Ear, Nose and Throat Hospital in London where they have his records and could not account for his astonishing, instant cure. The same test must be applied to the Bible.

Jesus is the focal point of the miracles in the Bible, and his activity stirred up all the controversy. He turned Palestine upside down with his compassion for suffering people. His miraculous deeds were so widely known that even the secular historians of the time recorded the things that were being reported about him. No serious historical scholar denies the existence and life of Christ. But Jesus never said these acts were important of themselves. He was not a magician trying to make a name for himself by pumping up the crowds. Instead, he taught that his miracles pointed beyond themselves to something more important—to who he was and what his mission was all about.

The miracles were recorded in the earliest accounts about Jesus at a time when his enemies, at the very least, could have denounced these events as fabrications. History shows they did not. Instead we find them seeking to explain them away as magic and sorcery. Some have even suggested that Jesus was using physical principles that modern science has yet to discover to perform his miraculous feats!

However, the miracles are not easily explained away. We cannot just dismiss these things as the superstition of simple, primitive folk living at the time of Christ—poor, ignorant, and easily fooled by trickery. People have never been stupid. Cicero, the Roman orator and statesman, wrote a hundred years before Christ, "There are no miracles . . . what was capable of happening is not a miracle."[12] Though most of us suffer from chronological snobbery (what is latest is always best or right), the idea that "people were less intelligent and more gullible back then" is a fallacy. The advancement of many ancient cultures is well documented, and there are many things about such civilizations that remain a mystery to us, even at a technological level, such as how the pyramids were constructed.

Today we are still highly superstitious, even in the West. From black cats, walking under ladders, touching wood, horoscopes, extraterrestrials, and Feng Shui to spiritualism, scientology, fortune-telling, crystals, psychic fairs, Ouija boards, tarot cards, and various other New Age practices, we are fascinated with the spiritual and supernatural. Does that make all of us stupid? People at the time of Christ were just as skeptical as we are about miraculous claims, and the Bible records many of the incredulous responses of individuals and crowds. They knew that dead people do not normally come back to life, or the blind spontaneously recover their sight. When Thomas, one of the disciples of Jesus, was told that some had seen Christ raised from the dead, the Bible says that he could not believe it: "I won't believe it unless I see the nail wounds in his hands, put my fingers into them, and place my hand into the wound in his side" (John 20:25, NLT). He became famous for this statement, later being given the name

"Doubting Thomas." Jesus did, however, appear to him and invited him to place his fingers into his wounds so that he could believe.

If we can accept that God exists, we need have no problem accepting the possibility of miracles. Paul once said to a skeptical king, "Why does it seem incredible to any of you that God can raise the dead?" (Acts 26:8, NLT). The generalizations of empirical knowledge that simply observe what "usually happens" can neither affirm nor deny whether miracles have taken place or not. If we look at the evidence for the miracles of the Bible, we find credible and thus compelling reasons to believe, just as we do for any other historic event, such as the victories of Charlemagne (Charles the Great). Open inquirers need not reject the Bible simply because it contains miracles. On the contrary, perhaps those miracles will move us toward understanding the Bible's influence, its power, and the authenticity of its foremost figure, Jesus Christ.

RELIABLE TEXT MESSAGE

It would take a tome to describe in detail how the Bible reliably records historical facts. This supernatural book contains numerous fulfilled prophecies and has demonstrated amazing durability. I will merely comment on some of the most interesting facets and leave keen students to read further for themselves.

The eyewitness accounts of the New Testament were written within fifty years of Jesus' death and have been handed down meticulously. The testimony of each writer agrees with the others even though there is no evidence of collusion. The New Testament books were circulated widely, and so Christian claims were well known by the Jewish and Roman world from Jesus' own generation onward. The faith spread so quickly that the persecution and victimization of Christians is well documented from the first century. It is significant that, rather than the claims of the early church being rejected as false, Christians were warned to be silent about the events on pain of torture or death. Given that people alive when all these things took place could easily have denounced the claims, it is noticeable that they did no such thing. Those who persecuted the faith could only demand silence!

History shows that counterclaims were not made, and the faith continued to spread despite the early believers being thrown to lions, crucified, or sawn into pieces. The secular writers of the time, including Pliny, Josephus, and the Roman historian Tacitus, affirm the biblical accounts in matters of historic detail. Christ's life, his reported miracles, his sentence under the Roman procurator Pontius Pilate, his crucifixion, and his reported resurrection are all well documented by the historians of the era.

C. S. Lewis, convinced of the trustworthiness of the New Testament documents, writes, "The evangelists have the first great characteristic of honest witnesses, they mention facts which are at first sight damaging to their main contention."[13] The Bible records the initial doubts of the early witnesses and the abandonment of Christ by his closest friends at the moment of his arrest, which hardly portrays events in the best possible light. They were later executed, most of them horribly, an outcome easily avoidable if they had confessed to their "fantasies and fictions." But they simply would not and could not deny those things of which they themselves were witnesses.

The accuracy of the copies of these accounts (the New Testament) that we have today is breathtaking. In 1948, when the Dead Sea Scrolls were discovered, scholars realized the unparalleled accuracy with which the text had been copied over the years, since this new find contained manuscripts from the first century. We now have about five thousand manuscripts in whole or in part, some copied fewer than two hundred years after the event. The oldest manuscript, dated A.D. 130 (a few decades after the originals), can be seen in John Rylands University Library in Manchester, England. By comparison, to support the fact that Julius Caesar came to Britain in 55 B.C. (and the evidence for the Gallic Wars), we have nine manuscripts, the earliest of which was written nine hundred years after the event! Put simply, the Bible is without competitor the best attested text of any ancient writing in the world.

You've Got to Be Digging

Archaeology, for some a fascinating subject, spells boredom to many. Yet studying the debris left by humans in the past reveals a great deal. The Middle East (the land of the Bible) is of great interest to archaeologists because of its checkered history and often well-preserved sites. This discipline, which helps to verify or falsify historic claims, is the greatest defender of the accuracy of the Bible. The great nineteenth-century archaeologist Sir William Ramsay was a skeptic of the highest order and determined to falsify the New Testament historically with careful digs in the Middle East. Commenting later on Luke, one New Testament writer, Ramsay wrote:

> I set out to look for truth on the border land where Greece and Asia meet and found it there. You may press the words of Luke in a degree beyond any other historian and they stand the keenest scrutiny and the hardest treatment. . . . Luke is an historian of the highest rank and should be placed along with the greatest of historians.[14]

William F. Albright, widely regarded as one of the great archaeologists, stated:

> The excessive skepticism shown towards the Bible by important historical schools of the eighteenth and nineteenth centuries, certain phases of which still appear periodically, has been progressively discredited. Discovery after discovery has established the accuracy of innumerable details, and has brought increased recognition to the value of the Bible as a historical source.[15]

The record in the rocks and rubbish of the past stands as a mountain of evidence in support of the reliability of the Bible and its writers, verifying their testimony. Far from casting doubt on the testimony concerning Christ, this science has been a witness for the defense. In the words of eminent archaeologist and expert on Palestinian archaeology Nelson Glueck of London University, "It may be stated categorically that no archaeological discovery has ever controverted a biblical reference."[16]

FORETOLD, FULFILLED!

Some people put a lot of store in the vague projections of their horoscope, are fascinated by palm readers, and have heard of the dubious predictions of Nostradamus' strange rhyming quatrains. But to those looking for a book that predicts future events accurately, the Bible has no peer. It has made hundreds of predictions that have been fulfilled. One of the most compelling reasons for accepting the divine origin of the Bible is this astonishing supernatural element. Perhaps the best examples of biblical prophecy are the predictions concerning the coming of Christ. These tell us the time when he would come, the place of his birth, the family into which he would be born, and the condition of that family at the time, as well as the reception that he would get from his people, the Jews. They detail further how he would die and be buried, as well as his resurrection and ascension (see Psalm 16:8-11; Isaiah 53; Jeremiah 23:5-6; Daniel 9:25-27; Micah 5:2). More than twenty Old Testament prophecies were fulfilled during the twenty-four-hour period of Jesus' crucifixion. Note that these were not "postdictions" (written after the events), but prophecies written down more than four centuries before they took place. Most of the circumstances of their fulfillment were completely outside Christ's control, humanly speaking.

Many other remarkable historic predictions are made in the Bible concerning peoples and nations that have been unequivocally fulfilled, and no biblical prophecy has ever been shown to be false—a unique record among the books of the world.

UNBREAKABLE!

The Bible has had many opponents through the years, but its influence has simply grown into every corner of the globe. Written off as myth by some and as irrelevant by others, the Bible has resisted relentless ridicule. Voltaire, the eighteenth-century French philosopher, predicted the demise of the Bible in the light of modern rationalism. Fifty years after he died, his old home in France was used as a storage and distribution center for the Geneva Bible Society. Now, two centuries later, the Bible is more widely read than ever before.

The Roman emperor Diocletian, following an edict in A.D. 303, failed to stamp the Bible out. The French Revolution could not crush it with secular philosophy (Rousseau, one of its heroes, converted to Christianity). The Communists failed to stamp it out with atheism and political ideology. One might well ask why this book has been banned, burned, and bludgeoned with such animosity and scorn. The great Reformation hero John Calvin responds in this way: "Whenever people slander God's word . . . they show they feel within its power, however unwillingly or reluctantly."[17] There is something in this. People feel somehow that the Bible's message calls them to account and therefore feel threatened by it. So powerful a book is it that monsters such as the Soviet dictator Stalin could not allow it to be read in public or in private. It confronts all that is evil in us and commands us to do right. Somehow the words of Jesus are too potent for us—not politically correct enough—and they require too high a standard to be allowed to influence modern public life.

A purely human book would probably have been destroyed by hundreds of years of brutal opposition. The Bible has never shied away from its attackers, and indeed Christianity welcomes critical analysis, for the truth has nothing to hide. Perhaps its unbreakable character has proved the words of Jesus true: "Heaven and earth will disappear, but my words will remain forever" (Matthew 24:35, NLT). As the prophet Isaiah so beautifully put it, "The grass withers, and the flowers fade, but the word of our God stands forever" (Isaiah 40:8, NLT).

Sir Frederic Kenyon, a specialist on ancient texts and the former director and principal librarian of the British Museum, wrote shortly before his death:

> The interval between the dates of original composition [of the Gospel records] and the earliest extant evidence becomes so small as to be in fact negligible, and the last foundation for any doubt that the scriptures have come down to us substantially as they were written has now been removed. Both the authenticity and the general integrity of the books of the New Testament may be regarded as finally established.[18]

Viewing all these things together leads us to conclude that at the very least we must take the Bible and its message with the utmost seriousness. We cannot dismiss it as myth, fantasy, or fable. These are eyewitness accounts of events. In the final analysis, it is up to us whether we believe Jesus' claims about himself or not, but let us make no mistake about what he claimed and the authenticity of the documents that record it.

CHANGING OUR SPOTS

Ultimately, the most visible evidence for the truth of the Bible lies in the changed lives of those who embrace its message. Talk of reliable texts and compelling archaeology may convince the mind but do not often touch the heart. If the message is true, surely it will work in practice. Millions of Christians around the world confirm that it does. The God whom we meet in its pages, most wonderfully in the person of Christ, speaks to us personally and meets us where we are. The Lord Jesus offers not simply moral ethics, but himself, the Son of God, in relationship, to change us from the inside out. Consequently, when we look in the Bible we see ourselves, as if in a mirror, as it describes us and our failures and points us to God by whose power we can be transformed.

I have yet to meet a person whose life was in a terrible mess who claimed that atheism suddenly revealed a truth that changed his or her life for lasting good. Can any philosophy devoid of the true God bring hope and restoration? Can atheism give new life?

The message of the Bible mends broken lives and has the power to transform society, not by pointing us to ink on a page, but to the God it reveals. Empty ideologies leave us spiritually starved, but Jesus said, "I am the bread of life" (John 6:35), and the proof is in the eating.

A SUMMARY OF THE ARGUMENT FOR THE BIBLE'S DIVINE INSPIRATION

1. God exists.
2. The New Testament is a reliable document.
3. The possibility of miracles cannot be logically ruled out.
4. Well-attested miracles of Jesus Christ confirm his claim to being God.
5. What God teaches is true.
6. Jesus affirmed the truth of the Old Testament and by implication the New Testament.

7

The Big Story!

We were not made primarily that we may love God (though we were made for that too) but that God may love us, that we may become the objects in which the Divine love may rest "well-pleased." To ask that God's love should be content with us as we are is to ask that God should cease to be God: because he is what he is, his love must, in the nature of things, be impeded and repelled, by certain stains in our present character, and because he already loves us he must labor to make us lovable.

C. S. LEWIS,
THE PROBLEM OF PAIN

The heart of the sons of men is full of evil, and madness is in their heart while they live.

ECCLESIASTES 9:3, KJV

CARBON AND CREATION

In modern society it is often considered arrogant and intolerant to suggest that any individual or group knows the truth about the world. But as we have seen already, truth is inescapable. To reject any worldview is simply to counter it with your own, whatever that may be, or however undeveloped in your own mind. The question is simply, which account of the universe is true? We have looked at the atheistic evolutionist's and humanist's big story about the human condition, which is summarized by Oxford zoologist and atheist Richard Dawkins:

> If the universe were just electrons and selfish genes, meaningless tragedies . . . are exactly what we should expect, along with equally meaningless good fortune. Such a universe would be neither evil nor good in intention. . . . In a universe of blind physical forces and genetic replication, some people are going to get hurt, other people are going to get lucky, and you won't find any rhyme or reason in it, nor any justice. The universe we observe has precisely the properties we should expect if there is, at bottom, no design, no purpose, no evil and no good, nothing but blind pitiless indifference.[1]

The question is, how can we speak of "selfish" genes—which conveys a moral character trait—if there is no category of good and evil to make the concept meaningful? How can we refer to "justice" in a moral vacuum? In what sense can we speak of pitilessness without a comprehension of what we mean by pity? Dawkins's statement assumes these are opposites; yet in the same breath he claims they do not exist; so does this statement mean anything? If we are just the interaction of "blind physical forces," how our self-conscious minds could know this is a mystery!

However, despite all its problems (for example, how people could see the destruction of thousands of lives in the World Trade Center as neither good nor evil), this is the big story of a godless philosophy. Admittedly, if God does not exist, then neither do objective moral values. But we are conscious that objective moral values do exist; therefore we can be confident God does also.

The account of the universe and the human condition found in the Bible and in the teachings of Jesus is by design and purpose with a holy, loving God at the heart of it. When we consider the vastness of space, when we ponder how small we are in comparison, and how much space seems to be wasted, we can find it difficult to believe that we are anything special or significant at all. Why so much room if there is just us? Remarkably, physicists now tell us that the universe is just the right size to contain enough carbon for the existence of life. Any smaller and life could not prosper! If the universe were downsized at all, we would not be here. There is just enough carbon to allow you to read this book! Now consider whether you are special. We are an amazing part of God's unique purpose—so important that God made the universe just big enough so that you and I could exist to know him. This is where our big story begins.

In the Attic

I am taking on a big challenge in this chapter. We are going to try to follow the plotline of the Bible from beginning to end, picking up in broad brush strokes the key aspects of its teaching about ourselves. As we hurry on, remember that we are looking for an overall picture, a view of life and reality itself. Ask the question, does it make sense of the world? The Christian thinker Francis Schaeffer illustrated this with an analogy that I have developed here.

Imagine that for the first time in a long while you are clearing out your grandmother's attic. You are busy rooting around in dusty old boxes. Soon you come across an old hardback novel that is slightly moldy. Opening it you find that the pages have been carelessly ripped out with only small parts of the text remaining on each page. In this condition there is no way that you will be able to piece together the story. Clearly at one time it could have been read and understood, but not now. As you continue your work, you find an old shoebox containing a bundle of pages tied together with an elastic band that have been torn from a book. These pages could be those ripped from the old book; so you carefully start matching up the torn pieces to the mutilated novel as though you are doing a puzzle. Sticking them in place you finally complete the repair. Now the story can be read, and it makes perfect sense. The discovered pages proved to be what was needed to restore the ruined book.

The damaged book corresponds to our troubled and torn-up world, which is filled with strife and tragedy—a world where something is wrong, but we just can't put our finger on it! The discovered pages correspond to the revelation of the Bible. Does it make sense of our damaged world? When we hold up the Bible next to the universe, do the pages fit? The key question is, can we now read the true story of the world?

A GREAT START

The Bible declares, "For you [God] created everything, and it is for your pleasure that they exist and were created" (Revelation 4:11, NLT). As C. S. Lewis points out, God created for the sheer joy of communicating himself, so that we might be the objects of his love and in turn that we might love and enjoy him forever. The Bible opens with words unparalleled in all ancient literature, "In the beginning God created the heavens and the earth" (Genesis 1:1). We read that God is the great, ultimate cause of it all, speaking our space-time continuum into existence. In the divine fellowship of the Trinity (three persons but one essence, just as matter, space, and time exist as three distinct properties, each inconceivable without the other) God's love for himself spilled over as the Father, Son, and Holy Spirit communicated the universe into existence. John writes, describing Jesus as "the Word," "In the beginning the Word already existed. He was with God, and he was God. He was in the beginning with God. He created everything there is. Nothing exists that he didn't make" (John 1:1-3, NLT).

Nothing came to be through random chaos, but with unlimited power and perfect wisdom the triune God brought into being all that exists outside himself. We read that God made it all good, pronouncing his work "very good." All that God made was perfect—without defect, uncorrupted, and beautiful. The pinnacle of God's creative work was fashioning human beings. The historical biblical account tells us, "So God created people in his own image; God patterned them after himself; male and female he created them" (Genesis 1:27, NLT).

This means that there was a qualitative difference between human beings, the rest of creation, and the animal kingdom. Though fashioned from the same raw material with obvious structural similarities, humans were something more. No other creature was made in God's image. We read that God "breathed . . . life" into human beings: "And the LORD God formed a man's body from the dust of the ground and breathed into it the breath of life. And the man became a living person [or soul]" (Genesis 2:7, NLT).

We were made peerless to reflect the character and nature of God. Just as we can see our image reflected in a clear pool of water, so we were made to reflect God. Both morally, in the exercise of our will, as spiritual beings with living souls, and as physical beings with marvelous bodies, we were majestically created to reflect the nature of our Maker.

All failure to respect the sanctity of life, the nobility of human beings, and the intrinsic preciousness of every soul stems from an impoverished understanding of the nature of humankind. Every person is a wonder of creation, made by God and for God. Evil is a great tragedy in human beings, because we were made so noble. Cruelty from animals is never considered morally evil, because they are not made like God. King David wrote in the Psalms,

> For you made us only a little lower than God,
> and you crowned us with glory and honor.
> You put us in charge of everything you made. . . .
> O LORD, our Lord, the majesty of your name fills the earth!
> —PSALM 8:5-6, 9, NLT

This is the great start to the big story. The purpose of God's creation was to display his majesty and glory, to share himself with creatures who were made to know him and enjoy him—made to love and be loved, to be satisfied with nothing else but knowing their God in an unending blissful relationship. Significantly, we recognize that the desire of the human heart is really to know and be known! Relationship and fellowship is what it means to be human. As the actor Tom Cruise is reputed to have said, "All the money and all the fame in the world is worth nothing if you're lonely."

A PERFECT MESS

An apparent difficulty immediately arises in our minds: If God made this world perfect and free from evil, pain, death, and suffering, why is it in such a state now? Why are our lives filled with fear, problems, and strife? Not only do we suffer actual pain, but we are able to anticipate pain in the future and even to dwell upon our certain death, adding a kind of mental torture to life. When we are enduring suffering, many "answers" can seem hollow; empathy and kindness go a lot further than intellectual explanations. But in order to grasp why these things happen and why the world is as it is, we must take a step back from our own situation to address the cause, not just the symptom. Christianity does not offer a sedative to make us feel temporarily more comfortable; it searches out the disease, reveals the infection, and provides antibodies!

The Holocaust is one of the worst examples of moral evil and human suffering. In Claude Lanzmann's book *Shoah* we read of horrific acts of brutality: "Once when the Jews asked for water, a Ukrainian went by and forbade giving any. The Jewish woman who had asked for water threw her pot at his head. The Ukrainian moved back maybe ten yards, and opened fire in the car. Blood and brains were all over the place."[2]

Human suffering involves us in uncomfortable feelings about God. We feel that we don't like a God who permits evil in the world. Some take that further and say that the sheer presence of evil in history means that God is unlikely to exist. Others think that an all-powerful God who is wholly good cannot logically coexist with evil in the world. Yet atheism offers no comfort or solution to the problem—it fails even to define evil and leaves us with cold indifference.

The fact that we cannot understand the reason why things happen leads to our sense of frustration, which arises from an intuitive sense that things are not meant to be this way, and indeed they are not: God made the universe "very good." It is also important to realize that raising a moral complaint about evil in the world requires an objective moral law in order to contrast this "evil" with "good" and make it a meaningful question. But as we have seen, if a moral law exists, there must be a moral lawgiver. So in a sense, the objection assumes the reality of the God it is trying to disprove.

Is an all-powerful, good God inconsistent with the existence of evil in the world? This depends on how we understand the attributes "all-powerful" and "good." The Bible affirms that both of these are true of God, but that they in no way contradict each other. So what is the Christian understanding of the almighty, wholly "good" God? The implication is that the created universe is the best that is naturally possible under God's moral government. The objection assumes that a *free* moral universe that was wholly restrained from wrongdoing could be created. This assumption is unsustainable.

To understand this, we must consider the nature of freedom. As we shall see, the Bible teaches us that evil entered the universe by the misuse of the freedom that was given to us. In the Bible, evil is not a "substance" that exists in and for itself; it is seen as a lack of goodness or a corruption of it. Anything that departs from the way things should be (as seen in the character of God) is regarded as evil. To sin is to miss the mark and come short of this standard.

Moral action, or choice, implies freedom. Freedom is the power to resist or to comply with any degree of motive or influence that can be brought before our minds. This means that while many things may influence our decisions (motives, dispositions, and habits), they do not determine them. The individual moral agent is the final reason for action. So freedom means that we are not compelled against our will to act. Freedom implies a choice between alternatives and the liberty to will either. So if we were to ask, "Why did God not create a world where there was no possibility of evil?" we would be implying that God should have created a world devoid of moral freedom—a race of inhuman automatons.

The objection also assumes that God can do the logically absurd. Freedom and compulsion, virtue and coercion are logically incompatible. If I say to my wife, "I love you" only because she is threatening me with a loaded gun, my words lose their significance. All virtues are considered virtuous because they are freely chosen. God's universe of moral beings is a free universe under a moral government of motives, not one of physical force. God's being all-powerful does not mean that he can perform nonsense. As C. S. Lewis puts it, "his omnipotence means power to do all that is intrinsically possible, not to do the intrinsically impossible."[3] Although nothing meaningful is impossible with God, there are some things he cannot do! He cannot make 2 + 2 = 5. He cannot cease to exist. He cannot make square circles. He cannot change in moral character. He cannot lie. He cannot break his word. He cannot sin.

So whereas it is logically conceivable for human beings to choose not to do evil and persist in that choice, it is not feasible for God to create a free and therefore meaningful world in which he can "guarantee" that people will always choose the good. It seems that for God to override moral freedom in his creatures would be morally wrong; so to create this hypothetical evil-free world may have meant compromising the greater good of human freedom. If God stepped in to alter all bad consequences from wrong choices, our lives would be a mere illusion. We would never comprehend the connection of cause and effect, we could not mature as people, and we would never take responsibility for our actions. For all we know, if God were to eliminate all suffering, a far worse evil might emerge and far less good be accomplished.

The Christian is therefore able to say that even though there is much evil that we do not understand, our God has reasons for permitting it—though he does not directly cause it. The God of the Bible is all-powerful and all-good even though evil is in our world, but he has reasons for allowing it for now. His omnipotence does not encompass nonsense, and his goodness is not just a general wish for people to be happy doing whatever they please; it involves influencing people to be morally good. Today philosophers have recognized that this common objection is unsustainable, although many of us still wrestle with it.

God's moral role as the governor of the universe is different from ours as governed creatures. His role is not that of a distant spectator. Crucially, in Jesus Christ, God does not stand at a distance from pain, but, by sending his Son as a man, he participated totally in human suffering. The Scriptures tell us Jesus was "despised and rejected—a man of sorrows, acquainted with bitterest grief . . . he was led as a lamb to the slaughter. . . . He had done no wrong" (Isaiah 53:3, 7, 9, NLT). God's response to our pain is located in the cross of Jesus Christ. Ultimately, the weight of good that will result from creation will outweigh evil, pain, and suffering. This is the Bible's teaching and the sure hope of the Christian (see Romans 8:18-25).

GOD IN UNLIKELY PLACES

Many good things can result from suffering and facing evil. Heroes are born in adversity, heroines in time of struggle. Love is seen as true love only when it is tested, courage only when we are tempted to flee, integrity when it is more convenient to deceive, and compassion when we help those who oppose or can never repay us. We cannot celebrate a victory until we have fought and won a conflict!

Pain can even be of benefit or serve as a teacher. Pain tells me to lift the piano off my foot, remove my hand from the hot pan, or take the grit from my eye. Mental pain prods me to ask forgiveness, reconcile with a friend, give to alleviate someone's suffering, and appreciate each day of life. Pain teaches me that time here is a gift, not a right, and to value it by living for things that matter. Pain can and does lead us to faith.

It was in a place of savagery and barbarism that Ernest Gordon found faith in God. His inspiring story is soon to be released as a Hollywood film. It began when he was taken captive by the Japanese in 1942. Though told that he was going to be executed, he ended up spending three and a half years as a prisoner working on the Burma-Thailand railway. For sixty years he has had the ordeal etched on his mind. But despite the brutal treatment and watching his friends tortured and starved, he was shocked to discover he believed in God more and more. His memoirs published in 1962 tell a story of faith, courage, and forgiveness.

Conditions were terrible; disease was rampant. On average, thirty men died every day. In total some ninety-four thousand died building the railway. Death was so familiar that at times it was easier for him to sleep in the morgue with the dead bodies than to sit in the sodden camp itself. He said savages were more reasonable than those Japanese soldiers. He saw men hanged from trees by their thumbs, stomped to death, shot in the back of the head, or filled with water and jumped on. He was forced to unload rotting dead bodies in the unbearable heat on a ration of one bowl of rice per day. Yet the more horror he saw, the more convinced he became that there must be another way to live.

One day a fellow Scotsman died and willed his Bible to Ernest, who had always been skeptical about religion and at the start of the war had been an agnostic. The Bible proved to be the turning point. He began to take God seriously and read the New Testament, finding that it made sense of the world and its mess. Within weeks he became the unofficial chaplain, praying with men and leading services! One day as a young lad was dying, he just held him in his arms and recited the Lord's Prayer: "Our Father, which art in heaven, hallowed be thy name . . ." Ernest recalls that that young man died in a state of grace and peace. It was faith in Christ that then gave Ernest the will to survive.

He organized a camp university and orchestra with old violins from the Red Cross and recorders cut from bamboo. He recalls, "It's amazing what men will fasten upon and what beauty can be made from garbage."[4] The stunned guards heard them playing Schubert's *Unfinished Symphony* over and over. In September 1945 they were finally liberated. The guards just vanished; so the survivors climbed to the top of the nearest hill.

On his return home Ernest was admitted to a hospital with malaria, hepatitis, an enlarged heart, and ulcerated intestines. Soon after his recovery he went to Hartford Seminary in Connecticut, USA. He loved the place; its vision of democracy and the less institutionalized church later led him to take up a parish in Long Island. He was a powerful preacher whose moving sermons on forgiveness deeply affected his listeners. He was soon appointed Dean of Princeton Chapel, a prestigious position, until he began work behind the Iron Curtain for the emancipation of dissidents, as well as accepting invitations to speak of God's forgiveness in Japan. Promoting the release of the film *To End All Wars*, *The Times* ran an article that included an interview with Ernest:

> The odd thing is how many of the POWs have made much more of a success of their lives than those who had an easier time of it. Surveys show that their marriages have been much more lasting. But statistics cannot tell us much of fears overcome, of the seeds of faith, hope and love which lodged in their hearts to flower later in the lives of others.[5]

One cannot measure the fountain of good that can spring up from places of unimaginable suffering, where noble characters are forged in the furnace of adversity as the human spirit trusts in God.

THE GARDEN OF GOD

The God of the Bible and the existence of evil, then, are not a contradiction, and we see that permitted pain can be used in God's wisdom to serve a good purpose. But how and why did evil and suffering enter God's good creation? How does evil affect us today? This is where we reach the great axiom of the Bible and its singular explanation of why things are as they are.

God set our first parents in paradise. The Bible refers to that wonderful place as "the Garden of Eden." They knew God as we know a friend. They enjoyed a wonderful life with their Creator that gave them perfect joy. There was no death, no suffering, no crying, and no pain.

God instituted a moral government of mind from the very beginning, creating us as free moral agents. Motives are the instruments that influence the mind; so God's government is made up of powerful motivations with sanctions that reward and punish. These are designed to influence the human mind in order that we will pursue those things that result in the honor of God and the highest happiness of the whole universe, especially God and ourselves. To do this, the most powerful motives and considerations are given to us, to help us keep that course and not ruin others or our own lives. Just as a good human government seeks to care for its citizens, it also punishes those who threaten to destroy or overthrow that government and its people. It does this with incentives. If we murder someone—breaking the moral law—we may be executed or spend many years in prison as a consequence. This is a powerful incentive to prevent murder, necessary because murder ruins the life of the victim and perpetrator, not to mention the wider family and friends of both, and it dishonors the law and government. Without appropriate punishment, wrongdoing would ruin any government and produce anarchy.

Obviously, it is inconceivable that people should be under a moral government without the power of free moral action. (That is why we have "diminished responsibility" built into our legal system for those who act without mental understanding of what they are doing.) We are fully aware that we are free because our conscience tells us some of our actions deserve praise and some blame. Because we are free, we are morally responsible for our actions and ultimately cannot pass the buck to another. This it what it means to be under God's moral government, and this is how it was for our first parents in the Garden of God. They felt the weight of moral obligation and knew that in putting God at the center of their lives they would honor him and promote their highest happiness and that of the whole universe.

So God set our first parents in paradise, and they enjoyed unbroken relationship with him. They knew and experienced the love of God, and this love was reciprocated in the form of worship and enjoyment of God that met the deepest needs of the human soul. In our damaged world it is hard to imagine what it would be like to live untainted by corruption or death, knowing our Creator, where even our own bodily appetites and functions are controlled by his will. As C. S. Lewis puts it, "His [Adam's] organic process obeyed the law of his own will, not the law of nature. His organs sent up appetites to the judgment seat of will not because they had to, but because he chose."[6] Humans ruled over the creation, and nothing harmed them. Hard to imagine, but this is how it was! There is an echo of paradise in us all, in our longings and desires; we yearn to get back to the Garden!

ASHES OF EDEN

Winston Churchill once said, "The further back you can look, the further forward you can see." Genesis (the first book in the Bible) encapsulates that very secret. As we look at how things began and what went wrong, it enables us to see why things are as they are and how the world will be in the future for humanity. Genesis tells us that something went terribly wrong. Indeed, the whole of the Bible, including Jesus himself, refers back to the Garden of Eden where paradise was lost. A disaster of cosmic proportions took place in God's Garden. In the ashes of Eden we find the birth of death and the advent of evil. This disaster has become known as "the Fall." It is the subject of Milton's classic, *Paradise Lost*, and has inspired numerous films. The Bible teaches that death and struggle, heartache and pain were born when Adam and Eve rebelled against God and sinned.

Sin is to act contrary to the ultimate law of the universe. All laws express the will of the lawgiver. That law of love is rooted in the character and nature of God who is morally perfect. It is neither arbitrary nor above or external to God—it expresses his nature. In paradise our personal God, the moral governor of the universe, asked human beings to act in obedience to him as their Creator and ruler, the one upon whom they depended and the one who defines right and wrong. But Adam and Eve at some point chose to do as they pleased, deciding to become their own gods. That is the essence of sin: to believe by thought or action that you are your own God. St. Augustine once defined sin as "believing the lie that you are self created, self dependent and self sustained."[7]

What the first two humans found so attractive about disobedience is a mystery, but we know that every motive was present to encourage them to obey. They were lords of creation, with only God over them. They had been told that they could enjoy everything that God had made, except—as a mark of love for and dependence upon him—they were not to eat from the tree in the center of the garden. It was not a magic tree. The test could have been something else; it signified an acknowledgment that they belonged to God and that *he* determined what was good and right, not them. The strongest motive was brought to them not to disobey. God said, "If you eat of its fruit, you will surely die" (Genesis 2:17, NLT). But someone tempted them, suggesting that God was a liar, that he was jealous of them and insecure in his position, that he did not really desire their good and would not carry out the penalty for disobedience. Again C. S. Lewis has put it well:

> Someone . . . whispered that they could become as gods—that they could cease directing their lives to their creator. . . . They wanted, as we say, "to call their souls their own." But that means to live a lie, for our souls are not in fact our own. They wanted some corner in the universe of which they could say to God, "this is our business not yours."[8]

Theirs was an ultimate act of self-will, a blatant attempt to usurp the natural order of the creature-Creator relationship. They turned from God to self as the ultimate end, which set up a defiant will in the universe that would not surrender itself to God. A cosmic disaster had been set in place.

ORIGINALS AND COPIES

In disobeying God, Adam and Eve committed the first human transgression. Their act was the original human sin, and it had dramatic consequences for the entire human race. When prime ministers or presidents declare war, they involve their entire nations in the conflict. Similarly, when our first parents fell, we all participated in the consequences. If I were a child and my father were to commit a terrible crime, the rest of the family would have to bear many of the consequences. While I would not be personally legally responsible for his crime, the family would be regarded in quite a different light by the community. Our good name would be ruined, and we would be fatherless. It is seen time and again in the nature-nurture discussion that criminality often flows from an environment of crime. Son often follows father, or brother after brother. Blaise Pascal wrote, "The teaching of this original sin and its results seems offensive to our reason, but once accepted makes total sense of the entire human condition."[9]

It is not easy to accept that we have been affected dramatically by the sin of somebody in the past whom we never knew, but as we begin to consider the Fall it does make sense of our predicament. Each of us has consistently repeated the actions of Adam and Eve in turning from God and his law of love to selfishness, choosing to make self our ultimate end rather than God. Adam and Eve may be the original, but we are carbon copies in every respect.

THE DEVIL YOU KNOW

Let us look at it more fully. Who tempted them to sin, and what were the repercussions? Throughout the Bible a personal, real being crops up. The Scriptures give him several names—Satan, the devil, Lucifer. This is another of those axioms in the worldview of Christianity that is a dividing line between its solution to life and all other solutions. Central to the Bible's message is that there is a struggle going on in the world between two powers for the hearts and minds of people. Now this is not dualism. The devil is not another God of equal power fighting for ascendancy with the Almighty. Evil is not self-existent and is not part of the nature and character of God; it results from the misuse of freedom and the selfish pursuit of happiness (albeit a twisted idea of what brings happiness) by illegitimate means—that which is not permitted under God's government.

A belief in evil and a spiritual realm is evident all over the globe. Even in the West people are fascinated by the occult. Hollywood is obsessed with films about demonic possession, spirits, and angels. People recognize that certain evils, which defy any explanation other than a spiritual force influencing them, exist. Many of us have at some time or another been disturbed by evil in a way that makes us strangely fearful. Playing with Ouija boards, visiting mediums, attending séances, and watching terrifying supernatural thrillers are popular yet dangerous activities today. Where did these ideas come from, and who is the devil?

The Bible teaches that God created other beings, known as "angels"—spiritual creatures immensely powerful who serve and worship God. They were also created with freedom of choice, although they were not made in the image of God. The chief among these created beings was the mighty, beautiful angel Lucifer. The Bible describes how he became full of pride, wanting to be like God himself and usurp his government. He rebelled against God; so God threw him out and banished him along with a third of the angels, who had followed him in his insurrection. Ancient mythologies are filled with distorted accounts of the fall of angelic powers, and unknown to most people, horoscopes have their root in the worship of fallen angels supposedly able to determine destiny. Most important is that Jesus himself referred to the fall of Satan in the Gospels: "I saw Satan falling from heaven as a flash of lightning!" (Luke 10:18, NLT).

The New Testament is full of references to Satan, who is consistently portrayed as our adversary, our enemy, and the father of all lies. It was Satan who came into the Garden at the beginning to tempt our first parents. The Bible calls him "that ancient serpent, who is called the Devil and Satan, the deceiver of the whole world" (Revelation 12:9, NRSV). The devil's goal from the beginning was to destroy humankind by breaking the power of moral government. He sought to introduce confusion, lies, rebellion, and destruction into the universe, and he has continued his attempt throughout history.

Embedded in the Christian message, culminating in the coming of Christ, is the understanding that there is a real and powerful personal devil, with many demons (fallen angels) under his control. This is an inescapable supernatural element to the biblical worldview. C. S. Lewis wrote in the preface of his popular book *The Screwtape Letters*:

> There are two equal and opposite errors into which our race can fall about the devils. One is to disbelieve in their existence. The other is to believe, and to feel an excessive and unhealthy interest in them. They themselves are equally pleased by both errors and hail the materialist or a magician with the same delight.[10]

While it is important to recognize that these beings are real and seek to influence us, it is equally important not to become obsessed with forces we neither fully understand nor can control.

PARADISE LOST

When Adam and Eve voluntarily submitted to the temptation of the devil to rebel against God, there were devastating repercussions. A judgment fell upon the natural world and human beings. Something was lost.

God's moral law had been flagrantly violated. He had been rebelled against. His moral government was effectively being mocked, although he had lovingly and specifically warned of the consequences. If he is to be true and just, if his law of love and government are to be honored and valued, he must follow through with the penalty. To ignore sin would be infinitely unjust, which is simply impossible for God. Without a penalty, wrong would not be seen as wrong, and God's commands would merely be advice. Sin must be punished to satisfy public justice. God had no alternative but to hold them to account.

Some of God's sustaining power was withdrawn. Overall decay (running down and final deterioration) set into creation and the natural order. For humankind this meant eventual physical death. From the moment we are born we begin to die. God said, "you were made from dust, and to the dust you will return" (Genesis 3:19, NLT). Death, overall decay, suffering, struggle, and disease entered the universe.

Our first parents were then removed from paradise. This meant that they were separated from the immediate presence of God. Sin caused separation and the severing of a close relationship. The wonderful repose they had enjoyed in friendship with God was lost. Humanity became Godless in that his glorious presence departed from them. We became spiritually dead in terms of our relationship and attitude toward God.

Humankind became inverted as self became the ultimate voluntary choice of the will, and not God. Selfishness, and not righteousness, became our first choice. Our human appetites tended to draw us toward selfishness and were no longer directly controlled by the will, but arose as situations presented themselves. Our own bodies and appetites seemed to rebel against us. Just as the root of a tree affects the branches, so the act of our first parents has affected our lives as their descendants.

Having listened to Satan in rebelling against God, we also changed our allegiance. Our first parents took themselves out from under the direct covering of God and put themselves under the influence and control of the devil. That is, we have allowed ourselves to be taken captive by him. Because we do this by choice, God has permitted this tyranny.

These were the serious consequences of the Fall—human beings bringing misery upon themselves and the creation. We have all perpetuated this and are held accountable for our own wrongdoing. Our own sin is counted against us, as we have abused our moral powers and freedom to serve selfishness, not God and righteousness. Although nothing prevents us from obeying God, we willfully ignore and reject his claims upon us. So we see that while we might want to blame our first parents for the state of the world, we have simply copied them generation after generation. Humankind was born free but finds itself in the chains of selfishness with its voluntary allegiance to the devil.

The Bible tells us that this is the only way to understand human history with all its tragedy. The Fall lies at the root of it all, which is where the rot set in. Sin and rebellion, fueled by unyielding pride, are at the heart of the human problem. Can it really be true of us all? A little self-examination reveals this pride at the heart of the human condition. The clergyman/poet John Donne (1573-1631) in a sermon delivered in 1619 illustrates this powerfully:

> Solitude is not the scene of pride; the danger of pride is in company, when we meet to look upon another. But in Adam's wife Eve, her first act (that is noted) was an act of pride, a harkening to that voice of the serpent, Ye shall be as Gods. As soon as there were two there was pride. . . . So early, so primary a sin is pride, as that it grew instantly from her, whom God intended for a helper because he saw that it was not good for a man to be alone. God sees that it is not good for a man to be without health, without wealth, without power, and jurisdiction, and magistracy and we grow proud of our helpers, proud of our health and strength, proud of our wealth and riches, proud of our office and authority over others. . . . And as our pride begins in our cradle, it continues in our graves and monuments . . . and such as have given nothing at all to any pious uses, or have determined their alms and their dole which they have given, in that one day of their funeral, and no farther, have given large annuities, perpetuities, for new painting their tombs, and for new flags, and scutcheons, every certain number of years.
>
> O the earliness! O the lateness! How early a Spring and no Autumn! How fast a growth, and no declination, of this branch of this sin pride. . . . This love of place, and precedency, it rocks us in our cradles, it lies down with us in our graves.[11]

A WONDERFUL PROMISE

We are all conscious of this moral corruption. We seem so easily led astray by our own selfish desires. We are an enigma to ourselves. Our weakest appetites and lusts can carry our wills despite the strongest convictions of our minds and consciences to the contrary. Going against our conscience produces a guilt we often don't know how to cope with. We act in moral madness by choosing those things that stand opposed to our own best interests, and so we play into the hands of the devil as he tries to ruin our souls.

Despite all of this, God made a wonderful promise to humankind even while he was pronouncing his judgment. In Genesis 3 God makes a promise and activates a plan of restoration. God is a God of love and mercy who longs to restore and rescue his creation. How could he forgive people and bring them back to himself while upholding his righteous law and government and not violating human freedom? How could he destroy the devil's work? The answer is the essence of the Good News. This is what the Christian Gospel and the message of Jesus Christ, his death and resurrection, are finally all about. It is God's wonderful plan of rescue and restoration from the consequences of sin and the Fall. At the time of human disobedience God promised a Savior: "You [Satan] and this woman will hate each other; your descendants and hers will always be enemies. One of hers will strike you on the head, and you will strike him on the heel" (Genesis 3:15, CEV).

This seemingly strange verse is the essential thread of the entire Bible. God is saying that as a result of the Fall and the compliant enslavement of human beings to selfishness and thereby to the devil, a battle has commenced. This conflict is the basic plot of the big story in which God is working out his plan to save rebellious people, while the devil seeks to destroy them by making men and women "children of disobedience" (Ephesians 2:2, KJV). Ultimately, God promises that one born of a woman will come and inflict a mortal wound on the devil from which he will not recover.

A PALACE OF PLEASURES

Jesus, in the Gospel of Luke, gives a fascinating description of the condition of people since the Fall: "For when Satan, who is completely armed, guards his palace, it is safe—until someone who is stronger attacks and overpowers him, strips him of his weapons, and carries off his belongings" (Luke 11:21-22, NLT).

According to Jesus, humankind is like a great number of people in a huge palace. The palace is controlled by a mighty prince who is heavily armed. It is large and has many distractions to entertain its prisoners, keeping them from considering their predicament. To all intents and purposes they believe that they are totally free—except in those rare reflective moments when they realize that something is wrong with the world. In the confines of the palace, misery, guilt, fear, confusion, and disappointment stalk them. In reality they have never tasted true liberty. This picture reminds me of the film *The Matrix*, in which the human race is unknowingly enslaved by a race of machines in a complex computer-generated universe. Occasionally a person becomes strangely conscious that there is something not right about the world. Some discover their world is an illusion, that in fact they are slaves. But will their minds be able to accept the hard truth, or will they prefer to live a lie?

Jesus tells us that the strong prince is Satan, who by deception holds the world in a place of ignorance and darkness. The Bible therefore makes reference to the dominion of Satan and describes him as "the god of this . . . world": "Satan, the god of this evil world, has blinded the minds of those who don't believe, so they are unable to see the glorious light of the Good News that is shining upon them" (2 Corinthians 4:4, NLT).

The French poet Baudelaire once said, "If there is a God he is the devil." In the light of his own internal struggles and those of the world around him, he questioned the goodness of God. But he was confusing, as we often do, God, capital G, and god, lower-case g. According to the Bible, the god (ruler) of this palace of moral and spiritual imprisonment is the devil; so in a limited sense Baudelaire's observation was accurate.

Ultimately, the problem that confronts us is not just certain sins or our internal battles; these are fruits of a wider problem. The real question is how we can escape from the palace of the devil and the darkness of our willful ignorance. We may try to climb the wall with politics and education, but these will ultimately let us down. In the final analysis, this is what high culture, philosophy, science, art, and sociopolitical engineering are all about. Surely there is a way back to a better world? How can we return to paradise? We do not phrase it like that, but this is what we want. Other systems, activities, clubs, and therapies may temporarily make us feel better, but the problems will eventually resurface because they are all within the confines of the enemy's palace. We readily see all the mess around us but are largely blind to its true cause. This suits our adversary because his goal is to prevent us from thinking clearly. And the last thing he wants is for us to consider Jesus Christ and the message of the Bible.

GETTING READY FOR RESCUE

So far we are a little short on good news! If Jesus described our true situation, what is the solution? Is there a way of escape? From the very first promise of God, the answer to that question has been yes. There is one way we can return to God, restore our friendship, and be objects of the special love of our heavenly Father. The first step is the most difficult. We have to accept that by ourselves and our own efforts we cannot be free of the consequence of our slavery to selfishness and sin or escape the palace of our adversary. By purely human effort we cannot put ourselves right with God or find peace with him; we need help. We need a liberator. We must accept this diagnosis and the bad news about our condition before we will accept the good news of Jesus Christ. The cure only makes sense when we understand we are sick.

All reasonable people will admit that they have done bad things, but even this is not sufficient to make us accept the need for a liberator from moral corruption and God's anger against sin. The judgment of God that "the wages of sin is death" (Romans 6:23) seems harsh to those who think that human beings are basically good and merely in need of some improvement. However, once we have understood how corrupted our own hearts have become and how morally depraved and guilty we are, God's fixed opposition against sin becomes a natural consequence and the proper outworking of his goodness. God's anger is not the vindictive petulance of a proud king bent on retribution. On the contrary, it is a necessary expression of his character that he be opposed to sin as the most costly thing in the universe that has spoiled everything it touches. If he is love and goodness, he must oppose sin wherever he finds it, for the good of all. We have to swallow our pride and acknowledge our failure, but this does not come easily. How common it is to live in denial. Actress Joan Collins, in an astonishing interview with the *Sunday Telegraph*, said:

> I have never done anything bad to anyone. Never. And that is one of the things I'm proud of—I have never hurt anybody. I have never been vicious about anybody, never taken any drugs, never tricked anyone; on the contrary, I can say that many, many people have done it to me—men, husbands, business associates,

lawyers, the list is endless. . . . I basically think that when one meets one's maker, if I do, there won't be anything I've done that I need to be ashamed of. Nothing.[12]

Sadly, even if all she said were true, she betrays her guilt with a telling sense of pride—that foremost of human transgressions—a deadly attitude of heart that poisons the soul and leads us to deny the most obvious and basic fact of human experience—that we are all sinful.

> A recovery of the old sense of sin is essential to Christianity. Christ takes it for granted that men are bad. Until we really feel this assumption of his to be true, though we are part of the world he came to save, we are not part of the audience to whom his words are addressed. We lack the first condition for understanding what he is talking about. And when men attempt to be Christians without this preliminary consciousness of sin, the result is almost bound to be a certain resentment against God as to one always inexplicably angry.[13]

When we have accepted the truth, we have made the vital breakthrough and rescue is just around the corner. We are ready for the cure, as we have recognized our condition. The Bible is not a message that will now tell us how to put ourselves right; rather, it is a declaration about what God has done for us and how we can receive it. Completing the words quoted earlier, "For the wages of sin is death, but the free gift of God is eternal life through Christ Jesus our Lord."

THE ESCAPE PLAN

From the dawn of time and the sin of our first parents, God has been weaving his plan of rescue into the tapestry of history. Once we understand our situation, we can begin to understand the great drama itself. History can be seen in two broad categories:

Our secular world history, which historians tell us has in many ways been remarkably cyclic. There appears to be little real progress as kingdoms rise and fall. Think of the nations that used to have great empires: Italy, Spain, Portugal, Greece, Egypt, France, the Netherlands. Great Britain is but a shadow of what it was. Knowledge blossoms and then vanishes away awaiting rediscovery. The learning of the ancient Arab nations and the philosophy of the Greek civilization were lost in the Dark Ages and rediscovered by Erasmus and others during the Reformation. The knowledge of geometry, mathematics, and engineering in ancient Egypt is well-known; yet some of their technology remains a mystery to the present day. The ancient Chinese knew about penicillin, though under another name. The examples are endless. Secular history has in many respects moved in a giant circle. There are times of military power and weakness, times of moral decline and moral improvement. There is nothing new under the sun, and humanity remains in its predicament.

Then there is another history that has been running alongside that of the world—*the history of redemption*. Here God is raising up One who will eventually fight our adversary the devil to bring about our deliverance from captivity. It interconnects with the history of nations and civilizations (our secular history), many of which play an important role in the Bible as it records historic details. The main plot, however, is the outworking of God's plan—"[the woman's offspring] . . . will crush your head" (NLT), the words that God had addressed to the devil back in the garden.

The offspring (or seed) of the woman is the thread along which we find all God's righteous servants in the Old Testament who heard and obeyed God. This is not purely a reference to the physical offspring of Eve, as there have been multitudes of those who have not obeyed God. Instead it is a reference to a spiritual seed, an attitude of heart that characterizes the children of this great promise who believe and trust what God has said. The offspring or seed of the serpent (the devil) again is a spiritual and moral category characterized by those who, in line with their "father" the devil (as identified by Jesus in John 8:44), submit to his rule and lies and oppose God's kingdom.

THE PLOT THICKENS

The thread of the conflict between these two spiritual and moral seeds runs throughout the Bible. It begins immediately in Adam and Eve's first two children, Cain and Abel. You may know the account. Abel worshiped and obeyed God as he required and believed the great promise. However, Cain did not and became rebellious. Jealous of his brother's favor in God's sight, he asked him to walk in the fields with him where he murdered him in cold blood—the first conflict between the two seeds. When asked by God about his brother, Cain made the famous response, "Am I my brother's keeper?" (Genesis 4:9, NIV).

We then come to a righteous man named Noah. The earth had become full of unbelievable evil and immorality that flourished on earth without restraint. Noah warned the people of the righteous judgment of God against sin and urged them to change lest God should punish them. The people mocked Noah for decades as he constructed the oceanliner-sized ark, before the great global flood came and "swept them all away" (Matthew 24:39, NRSV), destroying all except Noah's family of eight. It was this same conflict, the two seeds. (See Genesis 6:5—9:19.)

Then we find the great father of Israel—Abraham—and his amazing life of faith. He is given a gracious promise by God that through his descendants (the Jews) all the nations of the world will be blessed. The people of Israel, who are the focus of biblical history, were to be a model of God's truth and goodness. Through their descendants would finally come our Liberator, a Savior for all nations. Abraham believed this promise of God, and consequently Israel became a nation despised and rejected for its worship of God. They were hated and opposed by nations at every turn (and have been up to the present). Constantly we see the devil trying to lead them to rebel, abandon God, and worship pagan idols—the same conflict, the two seeds at enmity with each other.

Then comes the famous Moses—Prince of Egypt—a deliverer for the people of Israel from their years of terrible slavery in Egypt, which also gives us a picture of our slavery to the devil. Through Moses, God then gives the people the Ten Commandments. This is the moral law of love, representing the will and character of its Giver. God wrote on tablets of stone what he had already written on the human conscience, to reveal his perfect character and to act as a mirror for us to see ourselves as we really are—our thoughts, our words, and our deeds (see Exodus 20:1-17; Luke 6:20-42; Romans 3:20).

As we look at God's law, we see all his beauty and all our imperfections that, in his love, he wants to change. Created as we are in his image, our happiness, like his, springs from holiness (moral good). If we were all as holy as this law requires, we would see universal good, peace, and joy. The law was given as a rule of action to promote happiness and to reach and convince people of their need for a Savior. But even while God was giving his law to Moses, the devil was leading the people to worship idols made of gold. They consistently broke God's commands, just as we do; so the good law became a means of simply highlighting guilt and condemnation. The French atheist Voltaire once said, "The lips are slow to obey the brain when the heart is mutinous,"[14] and the mutiny went on despite God's kindness. Again we see the two seeds at war, the same conflict.

Then we see God raising up prophets (people to speak on his behalf to the people). They warned against sin and rebellion and reminded the people of the wonderful promise about the Liberator whom they called "the Messiah," who would offer life and freedom from sin to all people. The prophet Isaiah's words, spoken over seven hundred years before the birth of Christ, are familiar to those who attend carol services at Christmas: "The Lord himself will choose the sign. Look! The virgin will conceive a child! She will give birth to a son and will call him Immanuel—'God is with us'" (Isaiah 7:14, NLT). Incredible though the prophecy was, the people did not listen! As a consequence Israel was ransacked time and again and taken captive by foreign nations. At times this salvation history was so depressing that it looked as though God was going to lose. The offspring of the serpent seemed to be getting the upper hand—the devil seemed to be winning.

Then there are four hundred years of silence—no prophets since the last prophet in the Old Testament, Malachi, gave a message from God. Israel is then occupied by the Romans. Has God been defeated? Where is the Liberator? Has the devil won? No, thank God. The conflict was entering a crucial and in many ways final phase. As the Bible declares, "But when the right time came, God sent his Son, born of a woman, subject to the law. God sent him to buy freedom for us . . . so that he could adopt us as his very own children" (Galatians 4:4-5, NLT).

God's timing was perfect. The plan that was intimated for so long was about to be revealed: "Long ago God spoke many times and in many ways to our ancestors through the prophets. But now in these final days, he has spoken to us through his Son" (Hebrews 1:1-2, NLT). What amazing words! Consider how important this statement is, which summarizes what we have been considering. At last the Liberator, the offspring of the virgin Mary (the seed of the woman), has arrived after centuries of waiting. God has come to us through his Son, Jesus Christ. But the devil has not disappeared. King Herod, a rebel against God, tries to have the Messiah killed by murdering all the male children under two years of age in the region of Bethlehem. He fails to kill Jesus. Thirty years later, when Jesus' ministry begins, he is baptized by John the Baptist and is then tempted by the devil in the desert for forty days. Satan at that time offers Jesus all the kingdoms of the world and the palace of his rule if he will turn his back on his Father and worship the devil instead. But he fails to trap Jesus or stop his mission.

Inexplicably we then find the most loving man who ever lived being persecuted and despised by the religious leaders of the time, who even accused Jesus of being one of Satan's children! At the end of the Gospels, after all the peerless miracles, mercy, and teaching, Jesus is betrayed by one of his disciples for a bag of money, brought before the authorities, and then handed over to be crucified in place of a mass murderer named Barabbas. As onlookers mock, the Son of God hangs in shame upon a cross—the ultimate symbol of criminal punishment and defeat. Has the offspring of the serpent finally conquered, and will history be his from Eden to Rome?

ESCAPE TO VICTORY

The opposite of defeat was actually taking place. In fact, the Bible tells us that here at the cross, Jesus is putting the devil to shame, defeating him forever and releasing prisoners. Jesus dies and is buried and sealed in his grave on a Friday, but Sunday arrives, and he is raised to life on that third day, defeating death! He appears, raised to life, to hundreds of people, and after spending time with his closest disciples he ascends into heaven with the promise of his return in like manner.

This is the amazing historic drama of salvation and liberation, the very outworking of a promise that had been made thousands of years earlier, back in the Garden of God at the fall of humanity. The death of Jesus Christ, God's Son, defeated the lies and work of the devil and all that he had perpetrated against us from the beginning. The devil thought he had won. Imagine what he must have thought as he murdered the sinless Son of God, but he had not understood what God had revealed back in Eden. At the cross Satan's head was crushed (Genesis 3:15), and his power would never be the same again.

In his richly allegorical children's book *The Lion, the Witch and the Wardrobe*, C. S. Lewis gives us a glimpse of what took place. Aslan, the lion, has just been raised from death, and Susan, who witnesses this marvel, asks, "What does this mean?" Aslan replies:

> It means that though the witch knew the deep magic, there is a magic deeper still that she did not know. Her knowledge goes back only to the dawn of time. But if she could have looked a little further back, into the stillness and the darkness before time dawned, she would have read there a different incantation. She would have known that when a willing victim who had committed no treachery was killed in a traitor's stead, the table would crack and death itself would start working backwards.[15]

The apostle John writes concerning the purpose of Jesus' coming, "The Son of God was revealed for this purpose, to destroy the works of the devil" (1 John 3:8, NRSV). Jesus was clear about what his death at the cross was all about: "The time of judgment for the world has come, when the prince of this world will be cast out" (John 12:31, NLT).

The message is simple. There is no freedom from the tyranny of the devil and our moral slavery to selfishness except through the victory that Christ won for all those who will believe and put their trust in him. We can escape to victory, freedom, and new life because of what Christ has accomplished. The Bible clarifies this truth for us: "only by dying could he break the power of the Devil, who had the power of death. Only in this way could he deliver those who have lived all their lives as slaves to the fear of dying" (Hebrews 2:14-15, NLT). We need no longer be slaves to fear or slaves to sin that ends in death. We can be free from Satan's tyranny forever because the offspring of the woman has defeated the serpent. The adversary, the enemy of our souls, can have no power over those who have put their trust in Christ our Liberator.

This is an overview of the big story. The Christian message announces the kingdom of God and Christ's victory over sin and death, proclaiming that we can be right with God and have peace with him. This message has been proclaimed for over two thousand years and will continue to be until he returns again to take his children home with him. Then he will restore all that was lost at the Fall, making a new heaven and a new earth where righteousness dwells. At that time, the devil, who, though stripped of his authority and power, continues to lie, deceive, and undermine God's moral government, will be destroyed. Jesus himself will slay him with the breath of his mouth (2 Thessalonians 2:8). In that place there will be no more sorrow, no more crying, and no more pain. The old way of things will be gone, and the deceiver will be no more. The paradise that was lost will finally be regained, but it will be even more glorious than the one before!

In the next chapter we shall look at Jesus and his cross in detail, not only looking at what happened, but at why his death can put us right with God and how we must respond if we are to be a part of his family of free children. Having seen the big picture, let us focus on our Liberator, the gardener of paradise.

When Christ went up to Calvary
His crown upon his head
Each tree unto its fellow tree
In awful silence said
'Behold the Gardener is He
of Eden and Gethsemane.'
JOHN BANNISTER TABB

8

The Liberator

If the life and death of Socrates were those of a sage, the life and death of Jesus were those of a God.

JEAN-JACQUES ROUSSEAU

About this time lived Jesus, a wise man, if indeed one ought to call him a man. For he was the achiever of extraordinary deeds and was a teacher of those who accept the truth gladly. He won over many Jews and many of the Greeks. He was the Messiah. When he was indicted by the principal men among us and Pilate condemned him to be crucified, those who had come to love him originally did not cease to do so; for he appeared to them on the third day restored to life, as the prophets of the deity had foretold these and countless other marvelous things about him. And the tribe of Christians, so named after him, has not disappeared to this day.

FLAVIUS JOSEPHUS,
JEWISH HISTORIAN, A.D. 37-100

AN UNUSUAL CARPENTER

A Christian teacher recently visited a secondary school in one of England's cities. It was at Christmastime; so he thought it appropriate to remind the young people at the assembly about the most wonderful story ever told, the story of the birth of Christ. The pupils were remarkably attentive and seemed to enjoy his account of the dramatic virgin birth. Afterwards a boy of about twelve came to say how much he had enjoyed the wonderful story. To the teacher's shock he said that he had never heard the story before and had a question about it: "Why did Jesus' parents give him the name of a swear word?"

The degree of ignorance concerning the central figure in "the big story" is quite astonishing, particularly among young people today. The impact Jesus has had on history is immeasurable; yet it is a surprise to some that he is more than a word some use to curse with. An unknown poet wrote:

> *All the armies that ever marched,*
> *And all the navies that ever sailed,*
> *And all the parliaments that ever sat,*
> *And all the kings that ever reigned,*
> *Put together,*
> *Have not affected the life of man*
>   *upon the earth as powerfully,*
> *As that one solitary life.*

Who was this extraordinary carpenter, and why was he here? Perhaps that is the question of all questions. Surely nobody has ever spoken the way he did or lived the way he did. He is the most powerful and evocative figure in history. Around twelve billion people have come and gone on this planet, but who has ever come close to being like the person of Jesus Christ? Hate him or love him, worship or spurn him, the one thing you cannot do is ignore him. Every day we affirm his unique place. He shattered history into two halves, so that whenever we write a check or note the date, we are measuring from the time of his birth. He is in every sense the centerpiece of history, and we are still fascinated by him. Popular books, films, debates, websites, and songs still feature him more than any other figure. *Time* magazine described him as "the most persistent symbol of purity, selflessness and brotherly love in the history of man."

Let us take a look at the *curriculum vitae* of Jesus Christ.

Born:	In a borrowed stable amid cow manure and livestock.
Mother:	Peasant girl, Mary.
Father (not biological):	Local handyman, Joseph.
Place of residence:	A small village of questionable repute in southern Galilee.
College education:	None.
Vocation:	Carpentry, until the age of thirty when he became a traveling teacher.
Public offices held:	None.
Property or assets:	None.
Published work:	None.
Television appearances:	None.
Travel experience:	No more than two hundred miles from his own home.
Natural dependents:	None (in the biological sense).
Death:	By crucifixion as a criminal in place of a murderer, approximately A.D. 33.
Burial place:	A sympathizer's tomb.

Would you have employed this man? It doesn't make very impressive reading so far.

Other qualifications:	Sublime teacher; miracle-worker, including walking on water, healing the blind and crippled, and bringing dead people back to life.
Other relevant experience:	Was raised from the dead after three days and ascended into heaven.

The rest is history. Never has good news spread so fast or altered the face of the earth like this man and his message. The historian and religious skeptic H. G. Wells, in his five-volume work on world history, found himself devoting the most space to Jesus Christ. He wrote, "An historian like myself . . . cannot portray the progress of humanity honestly without giving Jesus of Nazareth the foremost place . . . men were dazzled and blinded and cried out against him. Is it any wonder that to this day this Galilean is too much for our small hearts?"[1]

Some have even sought to claim that Jesus never existed, that he is too good to be true. The philosopher Bertrand Russell embarrassed himself by stating that it was historically doubtful that Christ existed. Nothing could be further from the truth, given the authentic and extensive historical sources. His existence may make us uncomfortable, but it cannot be reasonably questioned. Rousseau wrote:

> Shall we say that the gospel story is a work of the imagination? Friend, that is not how one invents; the facts about Socrates which no one doubts, are not so well attested as those about Jesus Christ. At best you are only putting the difficulty further away from you, without getting rid of it. It would be more incredible that four men should have agreed to manufacture this book than that there was a single man who supplied the subject matter for it. No Jews could have hit upon its tone of morality.[2]

WHO WAS JESUS?

The Nicene Creed (A.D. 325) has stated the universal belief of the church down through the centuries—that Jesus was "fully God and fully man." The fact that he seems to some too good to be true demonstrates that while he was evidently a man, he was clearly not a mere man, but God in the flesh—immortality clothed in mortality.

All the great and "good" teachers in history have pointed beyond themselves to what they were saying. The focus was not themselves, but their wisdom. If we may call any man "good," this is what we should expect, as no man is perfect. But this was not the case with Jesus. He instructed people, "Follow me," not "Follow my teaching" or "Follow my miracles." He announced himself as the answer to the human dilemma: "I am the way, the truth, and the life. No one can come to the Father except through me. If you had known who I am, then you would have known who my Father is. From now on you know him and have seen him!" (John 14:6-7, NLT). Notice the stunning difference. He said, "I am the truth." Grammatically the statement does not work. One might say, "I know the truth," "I have seen the truth," "I can show you the truth," but who can say, "I am the truth"? Who can say, "I am the life"? Buddha, Muhammad, Plato, Gandhi, and Sartre never claimed such a thing. They all pointed beyond themselves to a philosophy, deity, or ideal.

When Jesus said, "I am the truth" (John 14:6) or told Pontius Pilate that "everyone who belongs to the truth listens to my voice" (John 18:37, NRSV), he was making an amazing claim. He was stating that he himself is the ground of being; he embodies the epistemological key to the universe. Truth is not an abstraction, or even something that just "corresponds" to reality; in the person of Jesus Christ truth is made known. He is ultimate reality! He is the source and fountain of truth, and more—of life itself. Christ does not direct us toward life; life itself, he claimed, is in him. No "good man" could say this about himself; only God could. If Jesus was not God, he certainly was not good. As we see in this remarkable statement, Jesus asserts that if we have seen him, we have seen God the Father.

Even in the light of such extraordinary claims, none has been able to find fault in Jesus, whether friend or foe. He is the only person who has ever made such claims and was taken seriously by his family, friends, and even enemies despite years of being put under the searchlight time and again. The power of biblical Christianity is not that these claims are argued with philosophical persuasiveness; it is found, instead, in a man whose peerless life and words silence our mouths, overcome our minds, and render us speechless. I suppose this is what we might expect if we met truth in the street tomorrow. What is there to say when the truth is standing in front of us? This was the experience of those early witnesses who, like the apostle Peter (then a fisherman), found himself dumbfounded in Jesus' presence and only able to fall at his feet, saying, "Go away from me, Lord, for I am a sinful man!" (Luke 5:8, NRSV).

The magnetism of Jesus, his moral beauty, his miraculous life, his transparent, perfect, and guileless character, is the reason why people turn to him as their Savior and Lord. The most recent estimate is that around 123,000 people become Christians around the world every day; in some places this growth rate is faster than the birth rate. In the Bible he is descriptively referred to as the Rose of Sharon, the Lily of

the Valley, the Bright Morning Star. He has been addressed by follow-
ers and angels in a way unlike any other human being, with titles that
could only be given to God: Almighty, Mighty God, Eternal Word,
Savior, Wonderful Counselor, Everlasting Father, Prince of Peace, The
Beginning and End, the Christ, the Son of God, the Holy One,
Immanuel (God with us), The Way, Truth and Life, King of kings, Lord
of lords, the Only Wise God! There never has been and never will be
another like him.

It is obvious from reading the New Testament that Jesus claimed
to be God, understood his mission as saving people from sin and
death, and accepted the worship of human beings as God himself. The
theologian Biederwolf remarked, "A person who can read the New
Testament and cannot see that Christ claims to be more than a man,
can look all over the sky at noon on a cloudless day and fail to see the
Sun."[3] Jesus forgave people their sin (something the Jews thought
blasphemy, because only God can forgive sin), he claimed to have
existed before Abraham (who lived about four thousand years before
Christ), and he told people that he alone could grant them eternal life,
because he was one with God.

Jesus was a man. He got hungry and was tempted, he wept, he
learned and worked; but he was more than this. He said he was divine,
coming from another world and bringing a greater kingdom. To top it
all, he claimed to be the final future judge of all people. Martin Luther
once exclaimed, "Take hold of Jesus as a man and you will discover
that he is God."[4]

A "TRILEMMA"

We are forced to recognize what Jesus said about himself and ask
whether or not he told the truth. But what are we to do with a man
who claims such things? Our options are severely limited. The choice
today remains what it was then: He was a deceiver, he was deluded,
or he is, and remains, divine. We must choose. C. S. Lewis summarizes this "trilemma" well when he writes:

> A man who is merely a man and said the things that Jesus said
> wouldn't be a great moral teacher; he'd either be a lunatic on a

level with the man who says he's a poached egg or else a devil of hell—an evil liar. You must make your choice; either this man was and is the Son of God or else a madman or something worse. But don't let us come up with any of this patronizing nonsense about him being a great human teacher; he hasn't left that open to us. He didn't intend to.[5]

This statement, though not pretending to be exact logic, has been widely quoted by Christian apologists because it cuts to the chase. The very heart of Christianity beats with the divinity of Christ. If it can be shown that he was a liar or a madman (or in some way deluded), then we can cast the Bible aside as Christianity dies from heart failure!

The only way to determine the truth is simply to go to the Gospels and some of the period's history. We find a man who is the paragon of truth to family, intimate friends, and the public alike. They all believed he was sinless and witnessed his life in its everyday expression. I shudder to think what my family and close friends would say about my failings. Could the seemingly most authentic man to walk the earth also have been the most prolific and outlandish liar, whose deception has flourished for over two millennia, carrying millions of people in its horrid wake? Or did he speak the truth?

Perhaps he was a deluded megalomaniac? Do his teachings and actions typify madness or insanity? Is his wisdom, authority, and magnetism consistent with mental instability? Go to the Gospel of John and examine these things; test his character. I am certain that what you will find is neither a delusional mind (sincere or otherwise) nor a deceitful demon, but the divine Son of God. It is certainly more rational to believe this than the alternatives. As Lewis sums it up, "Now it seems to me obvious, that he was neither a lunatic nor fiend and consequently, no matter how strange, frightening or unlikely it may seem, I have to accept the view that he was and is God."[6] The Gospels lead us to that conclusion. Toward the close of his account the apostle John writes, "Jesus' disciples saw him do many other miraculous signs besides the ones recorded in this book. But these are written so that you may believe that Jesus is the Messiah, the Son of God, and that by believing in him you will have life" (John 20:30-31, NLT).

Jesus presents himself to us as the answer to our search for life, meaning, happiness, forgiveness, and the knowledge of God. In defense of his claims, we can note several lines of support: his fulfillment of prophecy, his sinless life, his miraculous works, and his bodily resurrection (which we shall consider in the next chapter). He never pointed beyond himself, but drew people to himself as the very embodiment of all that is needed to meet the deepest needs of the human soul. But how could Jesus fulfill these promises? What was the means by which he could deliver life and forgiveness to sinful people? How was he going to unite us with God and draw people to himself? It is Jesus who gives us the crucial answer. He says, "'And when I am lifted up on the cross, I will draw everyone to myself.' He said this to indicate how he was going to die" (John 12:32-33, NLT).

CROSS TALK

A friend of mine was doing some shopping in his local supermarket and, while waiting in line at the checkout, noticed the cashier was wearing a striking cross around her neck. As he was paying for his groceries, he asked the young cashier a question that startled her. "Are you a Christian?"

Taken aback she said, "What do you mean?"

"Are you a Christian?" repeated my friend.

"Oh no," was the reply.

"Then why are you wearing a cross?" he asked.

"What, this?" she said, looking at her necklace. "Well, it's nice."

"But it wasn't nice," he replied. "It was horrible. That's a symbol of torture and execution you're wearing. If I was to wear an electric chair or gallows around my neck, would that be nice?"

The point is a good one. The cross was a place of execution for serious criminals, a horrific punishment that sought to inflict as much pain as possible during a very slow death. Crucifixion was a terrifying ordeal; yet the cross has become a symbol of dignity, self-sacrifice, heroism, and hope that has impacted art, literature, and music with its potency. Today, however, the cross is little understood, being worn as a piece of jewelry by those who have no idea what they are wearing or what it means.

Jesus made it clear that he had come to die; he predicted it specifically in detail several times. He was to be lifted up on a cruel cross in order to draw people to himself. Death did not take him by surprise. His life was not taken from him; he gave it up willingly. Nothing is clearer in the Gospels than the fact that Jesus was going to lay down his life for the sake of others. It is interesting that about four hundred years before Christ, Socrates said, "If a perfect man came to earth everyone would gang up and kill him."[7] This proved to be remarkably prophetic.

CROSS-EXAMINATION

Out of the thousands of people who were crucified by the Romans, why is it that we remember Jesus of Nazareth? What exactly happened to him, and why is it so important that two thousand years later people are still talking about it?

The Jewish religious leaders were unable to cope with the wisdom and authority with which Jesus spoke, and they viewed him as a threat to their place and position. He too easily exposed their hypocrisy and deceit. It was not long before they were plotting to kill him, as the crowds following him grew larger and larger. Finally soldiers and religious officials came to arrest him. He had just eaten a meal with his closest disciples and had spent much of the evening in prayer, preparing for what he knew was about to happen. As they arrived to arrest him in the Garden of Gethsemane, just east of Jerusalem, his friends ran off in fear. He had been betrayed by one of his own disciples for thirty pieces of silver and was identified by his betrayer with a kiss of greeting. An indisputable historic fact was about to unfold: the crucifixion of Jesus the Nazarene by permission of the Roman procurator, Pontius Pilate. The worst show trial in history was about to begin.

His teaching had been in public, so he had nothing to hide. False witnesses were brought in to accuse him, but their stories could not agree; so the "trial" began to get desperate. Caiaphas, the Jewish high priest, finally asked Jesus the key question: "'Are you the Messiah, the Son of the Blessed One?' Jesus said, 'I am'" (Mark 14:61-62, NRSV). As far as they were concerned, they had little choice but to accuse him of blasphemy, an offense for which he had to be put to death. Jesus had just claimed to be God, which was unforgivable.

That was the end of his religious trial, but in order to execute Jesus they needed the permission of the Romans, for all capital offenses had to be sanctioned by the Roman authorities. Internal religious wrangling could not get Jesus condemned by a Roman governor; so they changed the accusation before Pilate to sedition against Caesar and Rome, accusing Jesus of encouraging the people not to pay taxes. They said he had called himself "the King of the Jews." So Pilate asked him if he was. Jesus replied, "My kingdom is not from this world" (John 18:36, NRSV). Pilate had several interviews with Jesus and could find no fault with him. So, after sending Jesus to King Herod, who beat him and sent him back, Pilate was in a corner. He wanted to placate the angry mob but also to release Jesus; so he offered to have Jesus flogged instead. But the crowd, whipped up by the religious leaders, demanded with great venom that he be crucified. Luke's Gospel describes the situation:

> *"You brought me this man as one who was perverting the people; and here I have examined him in your presence and have not found this man guilty of any of your charges against him. Neither has Herod, for he sent him back to us. Indeed, he has done nothing to deserve death. I will therefore have him flogged and release him."*
> *. . . but they kept shouting, "Crucify, crucify him!" . . . "Why, what evil has he done?" . . . But they kept urgently demanding with loud shouts that he should be crucified; and their voices prevailed. So Pilate gave his verdict that their demand should be granted.*
> —LUKE 23:13-16, 21-24, NRSV

Pilate washed his hands of the situation, having capitulated to the mob, and told the agitators that it was their responsibility; he claimed innocence in the matter. Jesus received a Roman scourging of thirty-nine lashes that historians say would expose the internal organs. Most people died after receiving it. The whip was made of leather and embedded with bone and metal. A crown of thorns was pushed into his skull, and his beard was pulled out. He was so badly beaten that he was unrecognizable.

After carrying his cross partway to the place of execution, he was stripped and nailed to the cross through his wrists and ankles. Cicero wrote that crucifixion was so horrible and shameful that a Roman citizen should not speak of it or even think of it. Pontius Pilate placed a sign above Jesus' head that read, "Jesus of Nazareth, the King of the Jews" (in Latin, Greek, and Hebrew). The religious leaders asked him to take the sign off, but Pilate refused: "What I have written, I have written!" (John 19:22, NLT). Even after the cross was dropped into the ground and the slow, agonizing death by exhaustion and asphyxiation progressed, Jesus was not left in peace. The soldiers and Jews insulted, cursed, and abused him, but he did not respond, except to pray, "Father, forgive these people, because they don't know what they are doing" (Luke 23:34, NLT).

Even in the humiliation, disgrace, and suffering, people were drawn to this man. A thief on a cross next to him came to his defense, both confessing his own sin and proclaiming Jesus' perfect innocence. Turning to Christ he said, "'Jesus, remember me when you come into your Kingdom.' And Jesus replied, 'I assure you, today you will be with me in paradise'" (Luke 23:42, NLT). Never did another human being speak like this man, even in approaching death. The Gospel of Luke records those final moments:

> By this time it was noon, and darkness fell across the whole land until three o'clock. The light from the sun was gone. And suddenly, the thick veil hanging in the Temple was torn apart. Then Jesus shouted, 'Father, I entrust my spirit into your hands!' And with those words he breathed his last.
> —LUKE 23:44-46, NLT

It was this earth-shattering event that led Augustine to say, "God has one Son on earth without sin, but none without suffering." Amid all the agony, Jesus called out from the cross, "It is finished!" (John 19:30). His mission had been accomplished, and he went to meet death. The Bible tells us that on that Friday afternoon, about two thousand years ago, death finally died, and what would happen over the weekend was a foregone conclusion.

SUBSTITUTED AND LIBERATED

The apostle Paul writes, "But God showed his great love for us by sending Christ to die for us while we were still sinners" (Romans 5:8, NLT). What was it that Christ finished when he died on the cross? What was the mission he accomplished? In what way was his death for us?

The cross fulfilled the plan of God that had been unfolding from the beginning. It was his means of forgiving sin and offering pardon, yet remaining just and upholding his government. Each of us knows that if we were to stand before a righteous God, we could not claim to be sinless. We know that perfect justice would condemn us. Right and wrong do exist, and no one needs to tell us that many of our thoughts, words, and actions accuse and convince us of wrongdoing. God, by his very nature, must disapprove of wrongdoing and punish it—no one could worship a God who overlooked sin.

We are all guilty as charged and stand condemned under the penalty of God's law. We have all rebelled against the precepts of his law: to love God and love our neighbor as we love ourselves. We have no means of escape from this unless some adequate offering is made that is acceptable to God. Something must cover our wrongdoing, yet satisfy God's justice and uphold the rightness of his law. The great promise of the Bible is that an adequate offering would be made, that justice would be satisfied and forgiveness extended. The death of Christ as an offering to God for wrongdoing is what the Bible calls *the atonement*. It is the way in which our sin was covered (removed) by the grace of God, but not ignored. John writes, "[Jesus Christ] is the atoning sacrifice for our sins, and not for ours only but also for the sins of the whole world" (1 John 2:2, NRSV).

Christianity is essentially this: If you truly trust (the Bible calls this "faith") Christ as your Lord and Savior, believing that he died in your place for sin and was raised to life, defeating death, the sacrifice of Christ is extended to you, and you are put right with God.

In order for us to embrace the fact of the atonement of Christ, it is often the case that we need to comprehend the reasons for his death in more detail. The idea of someone else dying for us and thereby making us right with God is difficult to grasp. Indeed, the apostle Paul says

that many ancient Greeks were confounded by this and ended up calling Christ's death "foolishness." But the apostle points out that
although it may at first appear foolish, it is in fact the wisdom and
power of God, which saves all who embrace it. It is wisdom of a higher
order—the wisdom of God!

If someone were to murder one of your family, the penalty of the
law of the land would (hopefully) be carried out. It would be unjust
to deny this and would make a mockery of the law itself to do so. The
penalty for murdering someone (in some countries, the death
penalty) shows how highly we regard the precept "Do not murder."
It is the same with God's moral government. The penalty for sin must
be carried out for God to be just and to show how highly he regards
his law. The final penalty or wages for sin is death (Romans 6:23),
which shows God's determination to uphold the rightness of his law
of love.

Yet, being not only a God of holiness, but also of grace, one who
wants to show every person his kindness and mercy, he did not want
to carry out this penalty on us. The Bible teaches that he wants to seek
and save the lost, that he desires no person to die in sin, but for all to
come to repentance (2 Peter 3:9). He longs to bring rebellious people,
even those who despise him, back to himself. In order to do this he
required a viable substitute to avoid the penalty's falling on us. But this
substitute could in no way devalue or disregard the precept and penal-
ties of the law. This substitute had to carry a morally *persuasive power*,
demonstrating and upholding God's holiness and justice, equal to that
of carrying out the penalty itself. The cross of the Lord Jesus Christ,
God's one and only Son, was the only solution.

When Jesus went to the cross, he was despised as though he were
worse than the worst criminal. He was beaten and insulted. Though
he came to save us, we spat in his face and mocked the very one who
made and sustains us. He was crucified; he, enduring the curse of sin,
though he had committed no sin, so that we (like Barabbas) might not
have the penalty inflicted upon us, took the death blow in our stead.
The cross showed beyond doubt the immeasurable love of God for us,
while clearly laying open the wickedness of sin and his hatred of it. It
shows the love that God has for us and for his law; the death of Christ

demonstrated both. The moral power of the cross is overwhelming when truly understood—that the amazing kindness of God toward undeserving people would lead us to repentance, the love of God would move and humble us, the unspeakable sacrifice of Christ would lead us to obey him, and we would find joy and peace beyond imagination in relationship to God. Because Christ came as our substitute, we can be liberated from the fear of death or judgment and can experience life in every way that God intended (John 10:10).

DO NOT CUT OUT THE MIDDLE MAN

The other crucial aspect of Christ's death for us is that he mediated in our relationship to God. He stood in the middle of two separated parties to bring reconciliation. Consider: We as human beings had violated God's law. So a mediator must be able to represent both God and humankind. Jesus, as the eternal Son of God, was able to represent the Godhead (John 1:1ff.). And in his humanity he was able to represent us, the ones who needed to be rescued. No one else could have represented both parties. We see the divinity and humanity of Christ clearly in the Gospels. As a man he was too weak to carry the cross all the way to the place of execution because he had lost so much blood. But as God he was powerful enough to calm storms and raise the dead! Paul writes, "For our sake he made him to be sin who knew no sin, so that in him we might become the righteousness of God" (2 Corinthians 5:21, NRSV).

It was essential for our mediator perfectly to obey the law of love. Jesus' teaching on God's law, the Beatitudes or the Sermon on the Mount, is the most amazing ever heard from human lips. To put us right with God he would have to be sinless, faultlessly upholding God's holy law. The apostle Paul affirms that Jesus did exactly this, as he was the only human being with full moral credit with God.

Sin works like debt: It builds up until we are "owned" by another. The only way to be free is to find someone who can pay the debt for us. With sin it could not have been another member of fallen humanity, as we are all in the same boat. It had to be the sinless, perfect Son of God; only the one who had no sin could be "made . . . sin" for us. This means he would voluntarily have to stand in our position and be treated as if he were the worst of transgressors. He would have to take the curse of the law for us. The sanctions for sin would fall on him. The prophet Isaiah wrote:

> But he was wounded for our transgressions,
> crushed for our iniquities;
> upon him was the punishment that made us whole,
> and by his bruises we are healed.
> All we like sheep have gone astray;
> we have all turned to our own way,
> and the LORD has laid on him
> the iniquity of us all.
> —ISAIAH 53:5-6, NRSV

Paul summarizes this clearly for us:

> Christ redeemed us [bought us back] from the curse of the law by becoming a curse for us—for it is written, "Cursed is everyone who hangs on a tree"—in order that in Christ Jesus the blessing of Abraham might come to the Gentiles, so that we might receive the promise of the Spirit through faith.
> —GALATIANS 3:13-14, NRSV

In bearing the curse of the law by freely offering himself to God as a sacrifice for sin, Jesus' sufferings were of infinite value to God the Father: His offering was for all people. The Scripture says that in this way, as our mediator, he made "purification for sins" (Hebrews 1:3, NRSV). Jesus' sacrifice satisfied public and divine justice and demonstrated God's mercy to the entire world. God's name and his law have been highly honored in Christ, and now upon the two conditions of repentance and faith (see the next chapter) God can safely offer pardon, without risk to his moral government and glory. So, as it is written, "having been made perfect, he became the source of eternal salvation for all who obey him" (Hebrews 5:9, NRSV).

The only question that remains is: Will we throw down our arms? After all Christ has done for us through his agony on the cross, will we accept the peace terms? Our substitute wants to be our liberator!

THE TERMS IN BRIEF

The forgiveness of God is free but is not cheap. He is always ready to forgive and to embrace us into his family, but his pardon cannot be abused. It is not a license to go out and live as we please. Christ offered his life to purchase our salvation. There is nothing we can do to put ourselves right with God apart from the sacrificial death of Jesus. We cannot earn it, and we can never claim that we deserve it. No amount of "good deeds" can reconcile us to a holy God. Christianity, unlike Buddhism or Hinduism, is not a system of karma, where perhaps, if we help enough people, the good karma might outweigh the bad. The matter of our guilt has already been determined. The cross of Christ was necessary because we already stand condemned for our sin.

All that God requires is that we repent and put our faith in Jesus Christ for forgiveness and the power of a changed life. Repentance simply means to change the mind and turn the will. We are in rebellion against God with a mind set ultimately on selfishness, neither loving God nor his interests. We are required to change our minds about sin and to set our will to obey the new Master in our lives, the Lord Jesus Christ himself. By his Holy Spirit according to the new covenant (contract), he establishes his law in our hearts, the law of love, which enables us to live a life of obedience that is pleasing to God, putting us at peace with him, with others, and with ourselves. Obeying Jesus' law of liberty produces a happiness that cannot be removed, because it is the result of holiness and is not dependent on outward circumstances.

Faith means not only to believe the truth concerning Christ and his death and resurrection, but also to put our whole trust in him—to throw ourselves upon his unshakable truth. It means to put all our confidence in Christ himself and recognize that when we trust him he can bear all our weight. If salvation in Christ is like a chair, faith is not just appreciating the chair or recognizing its objective reality—it is sitting down. If it is like a car, faith gets in and puts its foot on the pedal. Only by investing in God's truth will we receive the dividends.

Jesus never shrank back from disgrace or humiliation for you and for me. As Peter put it, "For Christ also suffered for sins once for all, the righteous for the unrighteous, in order to bring you to God" (1

Peter 3:18, NRSV). The good news about the cross of Christ was designed by God to impact us and draw us back to him. Jesus promised that his death on the cross would draw people to himself. God's love, generosity, and mercy are the basis of his atonement, because mercy has always been the great principle of his government. It is God's highest joy to forgive, and our highest joy is to receive. Jesus tells us there is immense joy in heaven when someone repents and turns to God (Luke 15:10).

Jesus certainly saves all who surrender and return to God. Pascal puts it beautifully: "Jesus is a God we can approach without pride and before whom we can humble ourselves without despair."[8] When we have humbled ourselves, the inner transformation that Christ wants to work in our lives can begin. True spiritual life and nourishment is now available. Ravi Zacharias writes:

> It is our being that Jesus wants to feed. Christ warns that there are depths to our hungers that the physical cannot plumb. There are heights to our existential aspirations that our activities cannot attain. There are breadths of need that the natural cannot span.[9]

In Christ we feed on bread from heaven that purifies and sustains our humanity, by sharing in life-giving fellowship with divinity. The Liberator invites us all to a banquet for the soul. Christ in us, the hope of glory!

9

A Rolling Stone

I have been used for many years to study the histories of other times, and to examine and weigh the evidence of those who have written about them, and I know of no one fact in the history of mankind which is proved by better and fuller evidence of every sort, to the understanding of a fair inquirer, than the great sign which God hath given us that Christ died and rose again from the dead.

PROFESSOR THOMAS ARNOLD,
FORMER CHAIR OF MODERN HISTORY AT OXFORD AND
AUTHOR OF THE THREE-VOLUME *HISTORY OF ROME*

"I am the resurrection and the life. Those who believe in me, even though they die, will live, and everyone who lives and believes in me will never die."

JESUS CHRIST, JOHN 11:25-26, NRSV

THE LAST ENEMY

The Chambers English Dictionary defines death as "the final cessation of all the vital functions." Everything living dies—plants, animals, people, and everything in between. The ending of vital functions is the ultimate statistic—one out of one dies! No matter who we are, what we have accomplished, how much money we have, or what our position in life, death comes to us all. When we are young, it is difficult to believe that we shall ever die; and even as we grow old, we find it almost impossible to contemplate our own death. But the truth seems a harsh reality: In the midst of life we are in death. By the time you have finished this chapter, about a billion cells in your body will have died, and approximately sixty people in the United Kingdom will have made the final journey to the undiscovered country.

Despite the fact that death fills many with uncertainty, fear, and even dread, deep down most of us cannot believe in our mortality. In some way we are convinced that we shall live on. Remarkably, atheists too can have a vague conviction in this matter. "While my personality may not live on," some say, "my spirit or essence might. I may be reincarnated or reconstituted, or even join other spirits!" For most of us, the idea that the person we know as *I* will no longer be goes against all our instincts.

I have often noticed that those who deny there is a God are usually fearful about death, insisting that personal, conscious life after death is mere wishful thinking. I have become convinced, however, that denial of God's existence is the ultimate evasion. Given our convictions about right, wrong, and accountability, it can easily be argued that the idea of life after death is dreadful for that very reason. Those who have consistently denied the reality of God—and lived as though he were dead—will hardly be thrilled about the idea of meeting their Maker to give an account of themselves. Is not the real wishful thinking to believe that, finally, we will merely get away with everything we have done?

Whatever we believe, one thing is certain: Death comes to us all. His arrival has long been feared. The Grim Reaper's harvest has been ripe throughout history, and he never has a bad year. Death is sharpening his blade, and time is his sickle. Finally the clock will stop ticking, and the enemy we have sought to outrun with medicine, exercise, diets, and cosmetic surgery will overtake us. The question is, what happens next?

Great Exceptions

There has been only one person in human history who not only claimed to be able to defy death and win, but was seen by hundreds to be raised from the dead, never to die again. The only exception to our ultimate statistic is Jesus Christ, the conqueror of death. One of his most famous sayings concerns death itself: "I am the resurrection and the life. Those who believe in me, even though they die, will live" (John 11:25-26, NRSV).

I find no sight more distressing than a funeral where there is no hope, only despair and sorrow. Jesus had arrived at just such a place of mourning when he said these words, and shortly afterwards he raised a man named Lazarus from the dead, demonstrating divine authority over death itself (John 11:1ff.). Later in life Lazarus died again, but Jesus was raised and ascended into heaven in a body that had defied death; he was not just a spirit, thus making resurrection claims falsifiable.

If the resurrection of Jesus took place, it is not only the supreme fact of history, but the ultimate proof that he is God and Christianity is true. The resurrection is the great authenticator! If Christ is raised, then the curse is broken. God had pronounced over rebellious people back in the Garden, "you are dust, and to dust you shall return" (Genesis 3:19, NRSV). We have seen this ever since, as we scatter the ashes of dead loved ones, to be picked up by the wind or absorbed into the soil. It can all seem so hopeless. But if Christ is the great exception, if his words are true, if he can give life eternal to those who come to him, then sorrow is at an end, the fear of death and the grave is broken, death's harvest has been ruined, and we are free!

Perhaps this very issue led the atheist Professor Joad to say, "The most important question in the world is did Christ rise from the dead?" No question is more important, because, if the resurrection is true, we dare not fail to acknowledge its implications. If it is not true, and Christ is still in his grave, then the last enemy, death, remains undefeated, the darkness of the tomb is all there is, and Christ is proven a liar. The Bible itself is clear about this: "If Christ has not been raised, then our proclamation has been in vain and your faith has been in vain. We are even found to be misrepresenting God" (1 Corinthians 15:14-15, NRSV).

Christianity ceases to exist outside the physical resurrection of Christ, and the early disciples acknowledged this; but they boldly proclaimed that Christ *had* been raised and staked their very lives upon it. Naturally most of us find the idea of resurrection incredible because we do not observe such things today. But is Christ's resurrection really as incredible as it may sound? Considering all he said and did, from his promise of life to healing the sick and raising others who had died, Jesus is unique, in a class of his own! If the events in the Gospels took place, then is it incredible that Jesus defeated death itself? The greater mystery is how divinity could die! The resurrection seemed inevitable. If Jesus had not been unique, and resurrection from death was a common occurrence, this event would hardly stand out in history. Furthermore, given that in the Christian worldview death is the consequence of sin, the sinless Christ *had* to be raised. If not, sin would have remained undefeated. But death and the grave could not hold him.

THE WITNESS OF HISTORY

Naturally, the primary sources for the resurrection are the New Testament documents, although mentions of the resurrection are also found in other sources of the period (as we have seen). It is virtually indisputable that the New Testament documents were in circulation within fifty years of the death of Christ. Mark's Gospel, it is reckoned (representing Peter's teaching), was in existence as early as A.D. 44. We have already noted the authenticity of Luke's Gospel as an accurate historical account of the period. The other Gospels have shown themselves to be equally trustworthy, with archaeology consistently supporting them. In the 1950s, for example, funeral urns dating back to only twenty years after Jesus' death were found in Jerusalem. On the urns were inscriptions referring to belief in the bodily resurrection of Christ. The New Testament beliefs were not legends that became embellished with time—they were the conviction of the earliest Christian believers.

The claim of the resurrection is a historical one that can be tested in the same way as any other claim in history, such as the conquests of Napoleon. If we have the preconceived notion that such a thing is impossible, we cannot call ourselves objective or rational, and we do injustice to the facts. The resurrection is outside the realm of scientific inquiry, as scientific method applies only to repeatable events.

We should note an important difference between the scientific and legal methods of determining truth. The legal method does not ignore testimony or facts because they are not reproducible or testable. By a process of elimination and corroboration this method allows history and testimony to speak for itself until a verdict is reached "beyond reasonable doubt" and the balance of probability is achieved. I did not witness the battle of the Somme during the First World War, as I was not alive then. I cannot reproduce or test whether that war took place; so I must rely on documents and independent testimony to determine its plausibility.

This is precisely what the lawyer looks for when seeking to convince a jury: evidence from witnesses, material evidence, and circumstantial events that give the testimonies weight. Such a line of reasoning led the Lord Chief Justice of England, Lord Darling, to say, "No intelligent jury in the world could fail to bring the verdict that the resurrection story is true."[1] Dr. Frank Morison, a skeptical and rationalistic lawyer, thought the resurrection was a fairy story until he looked at the evidence and became convinced that Christ was raised from the dead. He had originally set out to write a book debunking the whole thing, but ended up publishing a brilliant defense called *Who Moved the Stone?* He writes:

> . . . the supreme and decisive factor lay in the fact that, throughout the early decades of Christianity, the physical vacancy of the authentic tomb of Christ was not in doubt. Events seem to have conspired to place that beyond the reach of argument. . . . Whoever comes to this problem has sooner or later to confront a fact which cannot be explained away or removed by any logical processes whatsoever. It looks us persistently in the face as the one concrete and unassailably attested certainty of the situation. This fact is that, sometime between the close of the thirty-six hour gap (after Christ's death) and a period we cannot reasonably place more than six or seven weeks later, a profound conviction came to the little group of people . . . that Jesus had risen from the grave.[2]

All of the disciples, including those who deserted Christ at his arrest, experienced something that changed their lives forever. Just a few years after these events, the Christian church stretched from Jerusalem through Asia Minor to Rome itself. Yet the impetus behind this lay in a small band of men and women who had been hiding in fear after the brutal death of their leader. They were full of doubt and confusion and were about to return to their old lives when something happened that transformed them. A few weeks later, filled with a new boldness and compelling power, they were found in Jerusalem proclaiming the resurrection!

Four simple facts are well established by historical scholarship, even by critics of Christianity:

> 1. The existence of Jesus Christ—an unusual teacher and unique figure.
> 2. The crucifixion of Jesus under Pontius Pilate.
> 3. The empty tomb of Jesus (no body ever found).
> 4. The Christian belief from the earliest period that Jesus was raised from the dead.

The only question to be answered is, what happened between 3 and 4? Is there some mysterious explanation, or was Christ truly raised from the dead? Jesus had predicted his death and resurrection many times (e.g., Matthew 16:21; John 2:19; 10:17-18). He had sought to prepare his disciples for what was about to happen, but the Gospels show that they did not grasp what he was saying. The disciples expected Jesus to liberate them from the control of the Romans and saw the kingdom of God in a purely physical, governmental dimension. Even though a careful study of the Old Testament makes it clear that the Messiah would be crucified and raised from death, the last thing the disciples imagined was that Christ would rise again.

YARN SPINNERS

The New Testament is clear in its testimony that the resurrection was real. Witnesses never claimed to have seen the disembodied spirit of Christ or to have had a vision of him at night. On the contrary, some were so full of doubt that they asked to place their own hands into the wounds in his hands and feet to make sure he was not an apparition. During the time spent with his disciples after the resurrection, the New Testament records that Jesus ate breakfast with them by the Sea of Tiberias and broke bread with two of them at Emmaus (John 21:1-14; Luke 24:13ff.). He appeared on at least ten occasions to a total of five hundred and fifty people, including five hundred at one time (1 Corinthians 15:6). This testifies to a real, physical resurrection, as Jesus asked for food in their presence to assure them of the truth. In the final analysis we have only three options open to us in deciding what happened between the empty tomb and the proclamation of the resurrection:

1. A deliberate invention (a fanciful tale).
2. A widespread delusion (hallucination or psychological phenomenon).
3. It actually happened (the truth).

Let us consider briefly the first possibility. This is the most radical explanation, and few intelligent critics would go so far as to suggest it. The reason being, it runs against too many lines of evidence. Paul tells us that most of the original witnesses were still alive— around A.D. 56, which was when the majority of the early documents would have been in circulation. To maintain a story consistently among a now numerous community with more than five hundred living witnesses (all in on the fabrication) seems to defy all possibility. Surely the truth would have leaked out via someone over that number of years. Think how people react when told to keep something confidential. A close friend comes around and says, "Don't pass this on, but . . ." In no time at all, the secret is out! But there is no record of any counterclaim or belief that the resurrection was a hoax. More than five hundred witnesses, even when the Gospels were circulating, affirmed the veracity of what was being proclaimed. Think how that number of independent witnesses would influence a court case!

Consider also whether deliberate deception is consistent with the character of the witnesses. We might reasonably suggest that it is psychologically possible for one or two of them to have become slightly deranged by the recent tragic events and to have turned to invention—but all of them? These people gave us the most profound ethical teaching known, and they lived it out in such a way that even their critics had to take note. It is a psychological fact that deliberate lies betray themselves in the behavior of even the most practiced liar. Lies eat away at us and are not inclined to produce self-sacrifice and love. But these Christians were prepared to die and give their lives for the message they proclaimed. Who in their right mind would go to an agonizing death for a lie they themselves had fabricated? Bear in mind that many of the early Christians were thrown to lions, burned alive, or crucified for not denying their faith.

Furthermore, too many facts are presented to make this theory of a hoax convincing. What forger would record the doubts of Jesus' closest disciples or have a former female prostitute, with no standing in the community, as the first crucial witness of the resurrection? The accounts are far too true to life, lacking the ingenuity of deliberate fiction. However, the fact above all facts that finally undermines the invention theory is the reality of an empty tomb. Consequently, most attacks on the validity of the resurrection admit the sincerity of the Gospel accounts but explain the miracle away as a psychological phenomenon. So how does the fact of the empty tomb shatter the idea that it was all a big hoax?

TOMB RAIDERS

To cover up this "great hoax," the disciples would need to steal the body of Christ and dispose of it. This was the first counter-explanation of the empty tomb. The panicking Jewish leaders claimed that when the guards sent to watch the grave had fallen asleep, the disciples raided the tomb (the Jewish leaders then paid the soldiers handsomely to go along with the story—see Matthew 28:11-15). The one thing that this shows conclusively is that the Roman and Jewish authorities did not have the body. Historically, theft was the official line, as the tomb was undoubtedly empty. If they had the body when the extraordinary claims were being made and Jerusalem was being thrown into an uproar, they could have produced it and squashed the rumors immediately. Instead, history records that they merely came up with this story and ordered the disciples to stop preaching about the resurrection or be severely punished.

Consider a further problem. The Jewish leaders, concerned about Jesus' claims, requested that the tomb be guarded by soldiers in case the disciples tried to steal the body. So Pilate allowed a guard of soldiers to be sent to the rock-cut grave and sealed it with a huge stone (Matthew 27:62-66). The penalty for professional guards falling asleep on duty was severe. Roman soldiers were among the most highly trained and able soldiers of the known world and took their work seriously. Now, either the guards were awake and overpowered by a small gang of seafarers and women, later to report this fact, or they were asleep and had no idea who took the body.

Both ideas are comical. That they should all be asleep on duty or that a group of dejected fishermen and women armed to the teeth with nets and fish-boning knives overcame the guards is ridiculous. Moreover, the disciples were hardly the kind of people to do this. They had run off when Jesus was arrested and had been hiding in fear since the crucifixion. More importantly, Christ had taught them to be people of peace, not violence. Are we to believe that, like a group of mercenaries, they overpowered the professional soldiers and then, knowing Jesus' resurrection to be a lie, fearlessly preached this lie and then died, often horribly, in the process?

A "Faint" Chance

With the idea of the disciples stealing the body being so untenable, some have suggested that the deception surrounded Christ's death itself. After receiving a severe Roman flogging, being crucified by professional executioners, and his death being confirmed by a spear that was thrust into his side, some contend, Christ fainted at the cross but was not killed! He may have appeared dead but was in fact still alive. This is the classical Islamic response to the resurrection claims. Somehow Jesus revived in the coolness of the tomb, rolled away the massive stone single-handedly, overcame the guards, and found his disciples. This suggestion, hardly worth dignifying with a response, demonstrates a profound ignorance about either the nature of crucifixion or of human anatomy. Even the staunchest skeptic has to admit that a swoon theory is totally unfeasible.

However we look at it, even if the half-dead body of Jesus had accomplished all this, we still have severe problems. Christ himself necessarily becomes implicated in this gross deception. Is this plausible? Where did he go? How could the disciples have become bold preachers of victory over death on the basis of this? If any of this took place, why did Jesus not become more of an Elvis type of figure with rumors of the King still living on somewhere in Massachusetts? None of these speculations is supported by material or circumstantial evidence.

Several facts emerge from all of this:

1. Jesus was dead when taken down from the cross.
2. It is inconceivable that the disciples could have stolen the body.
3. The Jewish and Roman authorities clearly did not have the body.
4. The tomb of Christ was nonetheless empty.

The fact of the empty tomb is ultimately irreconcilable with an invention or hoax by the disciples; it simply does not fit the evidence. Even if the women and apostles had gone to the wrong grave, the authorities could have ended all speculation by producing the body or indicating the right site. Sir Norman Anderson asks:

> Why did they not indicate the true grave, or, in the last resource, produce its mouldering remains? Why, instead, this feeble story about the disciples. . . . The empty tomb, then, forms a veritable rock on which all rationalistic theories of the resurrection dash themselves in vain.[3]

Given the above facts and the evident sincerity of the eyewitness accounts, nothing proposed so far in history has plausibly explained the fact of the empty tomb. Either we accept that Christ rose from the dead, as recorded in the Gospels, or we hold that something unknown happened, based on philosophical presuppositions about the possibility of such an event rather than on the evidence.

A Hallucination?

The empty tomb is, however, only one side of the matter. The other is the reported appearances of the risen Christ by large numbers of people. If the resurrection was not a deliberate deception, then perhaps the whole thing was an illusion—these people were all hallucinating, deluding themselves, and believing what they desperately wanted to believe. What are we to make of this idea?

It is difficult to ignore or explain away the appearances of Christ after the resurrection. They are evidently the accounts of eyewitnesses that are neither legends developed over time nor lies devised in collusion with more than five hundred people.

At the very least, they are reports from people utterly convinced of their truth, which is largely admitted by scholars. So the only alternative left for those denying the resurrection is that it was some sort of psychic phenomenon induced by drugs, hypnosis, or hysteria (though this still does not answer the problem of the empty tomb).

Two things should be noted straightaway. First, only certain personality types are normally liable to this sort of experience; and, second, hallucinations are highly individualistic, because they involve the subconscious. The resurrection appearances occurred among a considerable number of people at different times and in different settings, each person experiencing the same thing. How can over five hundred people of different personality types, at different times, and in different ways experience the same hallucination? Several times they did not recognize Jesus immediately. Nor did these things take place during some hypnotic demonstration or via a medium; nothing like this was present. Jesus appeared among them as a living man—eating, drinking, talking, and in physical contact with his friends.

They were neither anticipating nor expecting his resurrection and were understandably shocked when he appeared; so the idea that visions were induced by great anticipation is untenable. When you look at the appearances of Christ to his disciples over forty days, never to be repeated again after his ascension, the idea that these were random hallucinations becomes improbable to the highest degree. Instead what we seem unavoidably confronted with is the unanimous testimony of the witnesses that the Son of God was raised to life by the power of God, and his battered, broken, and unrecognizable body was transformed miraculously into an immortal, spiritual body of flesh and blood!

PURELY CIRCUMSTANTIAL

We have looked at some of the direct evidence for the resurrection of Christ, but other considerations should also be taken into account. We might call these *circumstantial* factors. Circumstantial evidence is not necessarily unreliable. In fact, at times it can be more pertinent to a case than direct evidence, as it is difficult to fabricate. Five points particularly stand out as supporting the claim of resurrection. The first is the existence of the universal church that had its origin in Jerusalem at that time. This is surely not coincidence. I have constantly emphasized that Christianity is rooted in the facts of real history, and not in mere subjective teaching. Without these events it is inconceivable that the church could have been founded and have flourished in the hostile soil of the Greco-Roman world. Without the resurrection there is no Christian church. The existence of the church therefore helps to substantiate the resurrection.

The second point is the changing of the Sabbath from a Saturday to a Sunday. This is highly significant, given that the vast majority of the early Christians were Jews. The Christian Sabbath, meeting for worship on a Sunday, was practiced from the earliest time. This can be accounted for only by the fact that Sunday was the day of the resurrection. Closely connected to this is, third, the celebration of Holy Communion. This sacrament of sharing bread and wine as a picture of the body and blood of Christ is a celebration of the Lord's sacrifice until he comes again (Acts 1:11). But if there was no resurrection, sharing in Communion is a hopeless and meaningless practice: We cannot be part of the Body of Christ if he is dead. His broken body and shed blood would have accomplished no victory over sin and the grave, and he could certainly not be returning for his people. Communion would not be communion with God or with others; it would merely be a morbid memorial to a dead man who had inspired people during his life.

However, we know that this sacrament was part of the worship of the first Christian communities, not least because the Roman and pagan world, misunderstanding the celebration itself, accused Christians of being cannibals! None of this makes sense without the resurrection. The same is also true, fourth, of Christian water baptism. When people confess faith in Christ, as a public demonstration of their change of heart they are baptized as a physical picture of what has happened to them spiritually. Going down beneath the water represents an end of sin and the old way of life that is now "buried with Christ," and coming out of the water signifies being raised again with Christ to a new life of freedom in God. Baptism in the New Testament and in subsequent church history becomes senseless without the resurrection.

Finally, the transformation of those first believers and the subsequent success of the church is inexplicable apart from the resurrection. Sir Norman Anderson puts it well:

> What, too, of the apostles themselves? What can have changed a little company of sad and defeated cowards into a band of irresistible missionaries who turned the world upside down and whom no opposition could deter? What changed Peter from a weakling who denied his Lord before a servant girl's questionings into a man who could not be silenced by the whole Sanhedrin? Paul and the evangelists give us part of the explanation: "He appeared unto Peter." What changed James, the Lord's human and by no means sympathetic brother, into the acknowledged leader of the Jerusalem church, all in the space of a few short years? We are told, "He appeared unto James." What else could have induced this erstwhile critic to write of his brother as "the Lord of glory"? And what of Paul the persecutor (who must have known all the facts about Joseph's tomb), and Stephen the martyr, and a multitude of other witnesses . . . and what of Christian experience down through the ages?[4]

As Simon Greenleaf, one of the finest legal minds in American history and a developer of Harvard Law School, remarked, "It was therefore impossible that they could have persisted in affirming the truths they have narrated, had not Jesus actually risen from the dead, and had they not known this fact as certainly as they knew any other fact."[5]

A ROLLING STONE

One Sunday morning about two thousand years ago, in a garden tomb near a place called Golgotha, men guarding the tomb were gripped with fear as they saw its covering stone rolled away. By that stone stood two angels dressed in dazzling white, and the guards ran off in fear. In that place the greatest moment in history had unfolded, and the divine plan had been completed. The lives of the first witnesses were about to change forever, and so was human history. To the present day, millions of people are still saying, "I know the resurrected Lord Jesus Christ, and he has changed my life! You can meet him too!" There has only ever been one victor over death.

> *There was no grave grave enough*
> *To ground me*
> *To mound me*
> *I broke the balm then slit the shroud*
> *Wound round me*
> *That bound me*
>
> *There was no death dead enough to dull me*
> *to cull me*
> *I snapped the snake and waned his war*
> *to lull me*
> *to null me*
>
> *There was no cross cross enough*
> *to nil me*
> *to still me*
> *I hung as gold that bled, and bloomed*
> *A rose that rose and pried the tomb*
> *Away from Satan's willful doom*
> *There was no cross, death, grave*
> *or room*
> *to hold me.*[6]

We saw at the beginning of this chapter that if Christ was raised from the dead, this authenticates all that he said. "The big story" is proven true and demands that we make a response. We dare not leave

Christ's commands unheeded; we cannot ignore what confronts us—we must act. History plausibly shows beyond reasonable doubt that Christ was raised from the dead, that he is indeed the Son of the living God. Surely the only response we can make is to heed his command to doubting Thomas ("Do not doubt but believe") and when finally confronted with Christ, the living truth, confess as Thomas did, "My Lord and my God!" (John 20:27-28, NRSV).

10

The Great Bar

Who can measure the happiness of heaven, where no evil at all can touch us, no good will be out of reach; where life is to be one long laud extolling God, who will be all in all; where there will be no weariness to call for rest, no need to call for toil, no place for any energy but praise. Of this I am assured whenever I read or hear the sacred song: "Blessed are they that dwell in thy house, O Lord: they praise thee for ever and ever" [Psalm 83:5].

ST. AUGUSTINE, *CITY OF GOD*

Nothing in all creation can hide from him. Everything is naked and exposed before his eyes. This is the God to whom we must explain all that we have done.

HEBREWS 4:13, NLT

FOOL'S GOLD

We are coming to the end of our journey together through the message of the Bible. We have seen many significant things along the way and have stopped to focus on the One who stands at the very center of it all, the One the hymn-writer calls "Fairest Lord Jesus." But in the end, why is all of this so important? In the final analysis, what does this mean for us?

The Bible explains, "it is appointed for mortals to die once, and after that the judgment" (Hebrews 9:27, NRSV). When our earthly lives are over (and none of us knows when we shall die), each of us will finally have to stand before God, at the Great Bar of Judgment, to give an account of ourselves. There will be no second chances, no reincarnations, no escaping our Creator. All that we have thought, said, and done will be laid bare before God. We shall be utterly exposed for what we are and shall have to explain the chosen course of our lives. That day will be one either of dread and terror or of irrepressible joy.

Jesus, in one of his many parables about judgment, shows the urgency and importance of recognizing the true nature of life and what the future holds:

> *"The land of a rich man produced abundantly. And he thought to himself, 'What should I do, for I have no place to store my crops?' Then he said, 'I will do this: I will pull down my barns and build larger ones, and there I will store all my grain and my goods. And I will say to my soul, Soul, you have ample goods laid up for many years; relax, eat, drink, be merry.' But God said to him, 'You fool! This very night your life is being demanded of you. And the things you have prepared, whose will they be?' So it is with those who store up treasures for themselves but are not rich toward God."*
> —LUKE 12:16-21, NRSV

Jesus' story concerns an ordinary man who has given little or no thought to what actually lies ahead; he has invested all his energies into the comforts of this life. Death and eternity simply do not enter the equation. His object in life has been to accrue things for himself—goods, land, and crops. He has done pretty well. So well in fact that he has to build larger warehouses to store all that he owns. He is pleased with what he has accomplished, and he muses on an early retirement. Now that he has built up enough capital to live comfortably, he decides to plan the years ahead of him as a hedonist—gorging himself with food and wine, parties and pleasures. But he has made a tragic mistake. This very night he is going to die. He will never see or enjoy his stored wealth, and in the end it will belong to someone else. His wealth is worthless—fool's gold.

Playing the Fool

Jesus calls this man a "fool." Why? He has spent his life on himself and ignored God. He was rich toward himself but had no treasure in heaven. He was selfish toward God and had played the fool. He thought he could presume on life, but he was wrong. With an impoverished soul, his life was demanded of him that very night; now he would have to face his Maker as naked as the day he was born.

Two of my close friends had fathers who were relatively successful businesspeople who, having worked hard for many years, planned to enjoy early retirement in the Mediterranean. Neither father had any time for God or the claims of Christ. Having made a tidy packet, off they went, dreaming of the wonderful years ahead of them. But within a matter of weeks of arriving in their new homes, both died suddenly; their lives were demanded of them. One of my friends, while attending his father's funeral, was asked by a guest, "Did he leave much?" My friend replied, "He left everything; he didn't take anything with him!" When Jesus told the parable of the rich fool, he was not just speaking about the wealthy. Many selfish endeavors can consume our lives: ambition, pleasure, notoriety, power, influence, prestige, and countless other drives. When pursued as an end in themselves, they are just other forms of foolish barn-building. Jesus was telling us that anyone not truly rich toward God, whoever does not place God foremost in life, is ultimately a fool. For as naked as we came into this world we shall leave it, and it is vanity to think that anything we have acquired or achieved for ourselves will mean anything then. If God is excluded, all is meaningless.

> *All streams run to the sea,*
> *but the sea is not full;*
> *to the place where the streams flow,*
> *there they continue to flow.*
> *All things are wearisome;*
> *more than one can express;*

the eye is not satisfied with seeing,
or the ear filled with hearing.
What has been is what will be,
and what has been done
    is what will be done;
there is nothing new under the sun.
Is there a thing of which it is said,
"See, this is new"?
It has already been,
in the ages before us.
The people of long ago
    are not remembered,
nor will there be any remembrance
of people yet to come
by those who come after them. . . .

I saw all the deeds that are done under the sun; and see, all is van-
ity and a chasing after wind.
                    —ECCLESIASTES 1:7-11, 14, NRSV

This is precisely why Christ called this man a fool. Only those
things we have invested in that cannot perish will outlast this passing
world; all else is like chasing after the wind. Jesus said:

"Do not store up for yourselves treasures on earth, where moth and
rust consume and where thieves break in and steal; but store up for
yourselves treasures in heaven, where neither moth nor rust con-
sumes and where thieves do not break in and steal. For where your
treasure is, there your heart will be also."
                    —MATTHEW 6:19-21, NRSV

Ultimately, what we invest our lives in reveals where our heart is.
The man who says he loves his family but never spends time with
them because he is obsessed with his work has greater love for his
work than for his family. This is something we all know to be true: The
things to which we apportion most of our time, thought, and attention reveal where our treasure in life is truly found. If God is not foremost in our lives, if he is not our greatest treasure, he does not have
our heart.

A FOOL'S REWARD

What then is the final reward for those who have played the fool in this life? What is God's verdict at the Great Bar of Judgment? Jesus tells another parable in Luke 19:12-27 to illustrate how God's judgment works within his moral government. He tells of a nobleman who is going away to be crowned king, shortly to return to rule his people. Before he leaves, he calls in ten of his servants and gives each of them ten pounds of silver to invest for him while he is gone. While on his way, some of his people send a delegation to tell him that they don't want him as their king, and consequently they become his enemies. So when he finally returns, he is eager to speak to the servants to find out what they have done with the money he entrusted to them to invest and to see if they have been faithful. In the parable the king only addresses three of the servants; presumably the other seven had openly become his enemies.

The first servant has made ten times as much as the original amount and is praised by the king for his faithfulness and is rewarded by becoming the governor of ten cities. The second has made five times as much and is also highly praised by the king and is given five cities to govern. But the third servant has made no gain because instead of investing the silver, he buried it in the ground. He was unwilling to invest his energies and time for his king and had done nothing with his grant. The king is furious with the lazy servant and orders that the money be taken from him and be given to the one who earned the most. The king explains his actions: "to those who use well what they are given, even more will be given. But from those who are unfaithful, even what little they have will be taken away" (Luke 19:26, NLT). In a similar passage, Matthew 25:14-30, the master then has all the unfaithful servants and enemies of his rule banished into outer darkness. What is Jesus teaching us about God's judgment in this story?

First, he is likening himself to the king. The Bible teaches us that God has given his Son a name above every name,

> *so that at the name of Jesus*
> *every knee should bend,*
> *in heaven and on earth and under the earth,*

*and every tongue should confess
that Jesus Christ is Lord,
to the glory of God the Father.*
—PHILIPPIANS 2:10-11, NRSV

He is the Creator and rightful king of the universe.

The servants represent us, the people being entrusted with precious silver. The silver represents the truth about God, his government, and salvation in his Son. Everybody is granted some knowledge about God and his government, even if only through their conscience and the work of creation. All are given some silver to invest. But as we are taught in this parable, people's responses differ.

The first servant is like a person who, on hearing the truth about God and his government, is faithful to it. He not only accepts it but invests his life in it. His time and energies are taken up with serving King Jesus. He fully invests that truth, puts everything he has into it, and gets a great return. The truth is multiplied in him and through him to others.

The second servant is like him. He too receives knowledge and understanding about God and the way of salvation in Christ. He takes that precious silver and invests his life faithfully in it and gets a wonderful return.

But the third servant is different. He is like a person who receives knowledge and understanding about God but does nothing with it. He recognizes God as the Creator and the giver of the moral law, and he knows his obligations. He is granted understanding, even of the way of salvation in Christ and how to be put right with God. But instead of investing in the truth and putting his heart and soul into it, he buries it, puts it out of sight and out of mind, and lives for himself. He thinks it's reasonable to know of these things but not do anything about them. He therefore does nothing at all with what he has heard.

The others represent people who flatly reject this knowledge and deny that Christ is King. "We don't want you as King!" they say, and that is that. They are not interested in the precious silver he has given. They reject him and never grow in an understanding of what God has done. Aware of the gift of God, they not only do nothing—they fling it back in his face. They "send a delegation," as it were, to spell it out to God: "We don't accept your government. We reject your plan of salvation. We defy you to your face. Consider us your enemies."

Jesus clearly teaches us that there is reward and retribution for these differing responses. Those who accept and use the precious truth that God has revealed are considered faithful people. Having used what was given, they will be given more, and more, and more! The rewards of heaven on the final day and on into eternity are beyond our comprehension. Jesus uses the image of being granted kingdoms to rule. But more wonderful than that, we shall "enter into the joy of our master" (Matthew 25:21, NRSV) "and receive the kingdom that was prepared for you before the world was created" (Matthew 25:34, CEV).

But those who do nothing with what they have heard and those who declare themselves the enemies of God's government and law of love will be thrown into "outer darkness," where there is only crying, anguish, and gnashing of teeth (Matthew 25:30, NRSV). This is the fool's reward. The fool's gold, in which he has invested, has corroded. In his folly he has pursued his own way, and his end is a death of separation from the King he despised. Jesus tells us, even implores us, in the Bible to flee this folly, for although the wages of sin is death, God's gift to us is eternal life in King Jesus—if we receive him and act upon his commands.

ENTERING THE KING'S KINGDOM

The apostle Paul affirms all that Jesus taught about the judgment of God and reminds us that "each of us will be accountable to God" (Romans 14:12, NRSV). We shall stand before the great bar and be judged in accordance with the understanding we have received and how we have invested this precious silver. Our consciences will justify or condemn us when God, through Christ, will judge the secrets of our hearts (Romans 2:15-16). This moral judgment we so often use to hold others to account will reveal our hearts on that day. It is not hard for us to accept the fact of accountability, because we sense in our day-to-day lives our obligations. We recognize that we consistently break

Christ's command not only to put God first, but in everything to "do to others as you would have them do to you" (Matthew 7:12, NRSV).

So when that day comes, rather than being one of terror and dread, how can we ensure it is one of unspeakable joy? There is one way only: Our consciences must not condemn us. But how is that possible? It is possible in this way alone: "Let us approach with a true heart in full assurance of faith, with our hearts sprinkled clean from an evil conscience" (Hebrews 10:22, NRSV). Our conscience must be washed clean; we must be set free from its accusations. Unless this happens, our time at the Great Bar will be one of despair and dread. The guilty conscience is the bane of human existence. A restless life is the fruit of a guilt-ridden soul. The Christian thinker Ravi Zacharias writes:

> What a vortex of human emotion swirls around this subject of guilt! We come up against it in our families. We battle for it in our courtrooms. We philosophize about it in the classroom. We try to explain it with psychology. We shout about it from the pulpit. We wrestle with it in private. So pervasive and deep-seated are its ramifications that some in professional counseling have gone so far as to say that guilt is the cornerstone of all neuroses.[1]

Guilt is the product of an unheeded conscience, but when conscience is followed, it directs us where we may be washed in the cleansing pool that is Christ.

CHANGING UTTERLY

Coming to be washed is the road to the kingdom of God. A purified conscience is the secret of a glorious day at God's bar of justice. How can we be purified and washed clean? The writer to the Hebrews has told us. We approach with a true heart in faith. Jesus put it simply: "Unless you are converted [utterly change] and become as little children, you will by no means enter the kingdom of heaven" (Matthew 18:3, NKJV). A true heart is a converted heart. It reveals a will that has been transformed—no longer *inverted* with self-interest, but *converted*, turned toward God and his will. This requires the act of repentance, a prerequisite of salvation. We cannot be cleansed from guilt while we are still in rebellion. That would be mean God's declaring sin meaningless. We must be willing to confess that we are in the wrong and that God is in the right. We must go on record, as it were, against ourselves, acknowledging our guilt and admitting our need for pardon.

In repentance our mind is changed toward God and toward sin. Those things that once enticed us, the wrong things we indulged in our hearts, we now turn from and see for what they really are. Instead we choose to love God and his holiness. As we do so, we shall find that the way we feel about God and sin changes in a corresponding way. Our emotions toward him and his law are utterly changed. To live in him and by his power, in joyful obedience, will become our delight—the deepest desire of our hearts.

This true work of repentance, though real and deep, does not mean that we who have become Christians are perfect, never do anything wrong again, or are never disobedient toward God. What it does mean is that the prevailing desire and ultimate goal in our life is to love God, placing him first, in obedience to his will. At the helm of our lives is a new captain. We have relinquished the rudder to Christ.

When a Christian disobeys, it should be the exception, because of weakness, and not the rule. The object of the will has changed; so we love and obey God, not out of fear of punishment, but for the joy of knowing and loving him. Christians no longer oppose God willfully, for we have embraced him as our friend and Father. Instead of wrongdoing producing terrible guilt and condemnation, in the believer it produces conviction—an awareness of failure and a sense of sorrow. This does not lead to fear and guilt, but gently draws us to God to confess sin and receive forgiveness. "If we say that we have no sin, we deceive ourselves, and the truth is not in us. If we confess our sins, he who is faithful and just will forgive us our sins and cleanse us from all unrighteousness" (1 John 1:8-9, NRSV).

THE FAITH FACTOR

God begins a new relationship with us when we repent and come to him. The Bible calls this a covenant, which has been sealed by the blood of Christ. This covenant is like a contract, the terms of which have been stipulated by God. Because of the death of Christ and the sufficient sacrifice he made, the covenant offers pardon to all on the basis that they repent and trust the provision God has made in Christ. This covenant promise is always accessible for any sin. We can never wear it out, never cause God to lose patience. The sacrifice for sin has been made once for all, and the repentant have endless access to the promise of cleansing.

The attitude of heart that signs this contract is called faith. Without faith, the covenant is void. True repentance is impossible without faith. Indeed, Scripture tells us that without faith it is impossible to please God!

The childlikeness that Jesus speaks of in Matthew 18:3 is the key to understanding the nature of faith. A child is simple and trusting, and Jesus speaks of the humility of a small child as necessary for entering his kingdom. Childlikeness should not be confused with childishness. We are not asked to ignore all that we have learned or to abandon all that adulthood entails. It is the simple, unwavering trust that a child has in his or her father, taking him at his word, that is required. It is not only to accept what Christ has done, but wholly and without reservation to throw our very lives into his hands and the strength of his promises. It is wholeheartedly to believe and act upon the truth we have heard. This believing heart toward God enables us to truly repent, because repentance is part of the activity of faith.

Faith activates and signs the contract. There is no small print, no escape clause, no hidden strings. It is not like some car insurance warranty that tries to wriggle from its commitment. God never breaks the terms—it is impossible for him to lie or break his word. It is an everlasting covenant, and faith ensures that all its promises, found in Christ, become ours. As the hymn-writer has put it:

> His love has no limit,
> His grace has no measure,
> His power has no boundary known unto men;
> For out of his infinite riches in Jesus
> He giveth and giveth and giveth again.
> ANNIE JOHNSTON FLINT

THE REWARD OF THE FAITHFUL

The great reward for those who come to Christ, repent, and surrender to him is primarily a gift. This gift is the most wonderful thing about the Christian life. The apostle Paul tells us what it is: "The free gift of God is eternal life in Christ Jesus our Lord" (Romans 6:23, NRSV). Now, we might think that the gift is eternal life; that is certainly a consequence of it, but the gift itself is greater than that. When we become Christians, we are not merely given a ticket that ensures our life will go on forever. The gift we are given is a new quality of life, the gift of God himself. He literally gives himself to us. The Holy Spirit comes to live in us, and there is a spiritual fellowship, a supernatural marriage. We are united with God in Christ our Lord. The apostle Peter tries to put this into words: "His divine power has given us everything we need for living a godly life. He has called us to receive his own glory and goodness! . . . that you will share in his divine nature" (2 Peter 1:3-4, NLT).

Peter literally means that we have fellowship with God's very life and character. Because of what Christ has done for us, we share in it—not only a new knowledge, but a new and immediate power for living. This indwelling presence of Christ enables us to become like him in our thoughts, words, and actions, keeping us at peace with God, with ourselves, and with others. So the great gift is the gift of God. Presents do not come any more amazing, satisfying, or lasting than that! Made as we are for God and to enjoy God, no other gift could or would be enough for us. Even unending life would not be precious if it were without God to give it purpose and inexhaustible wonder.

This is what the reward of heaven is all about: being completely satisfied in God. For the believer, heaven can begin now on earth; we can get a taste of it here. In the joy of virtue and peace with God, our soul finds rest. Sundar Singh, one of India's most famous Hindu converts to Christianity, poignantly reminds us:

> We are never satisfied with one thing for long. We always want to change our circumstances and environment. This restlessness stems from our deep inner awareness that the fleeting things of this world can never satisfy our souls, can never give

us a sense of stable and unchanging fulfillment. Only when we turn to the master will our desires be transformed, and perfect peace, the gift no one tires of, will reveal itself as the deepest longing of our hearts—indeed, the soul's only quest.[2]

The joy never fades, the peace never passes, the bliss blooms forever. Words fail when seeking to describe the future glories of heaven. Renaissance depictions of paradise, with saints sitting on clouds playing harps, are entirely misleading. The apostle Paul wrote, "no eye has seen, nor ear heard, nor the human heart conceived, what God has prepared for those who love him" (1 Corinthians 2:9, NRSV), and we know that Christ has gone on ahead to prepare a place for those who embrace him:

"Do not let your hearts be troubled. Believe in God, believe also in me. In my Father's house there are many dwelling places. If it were not so, would I have told you that I go to prepare a place for you? And if I go and prepare a place for you, I will come again and will take you to myself, so that where I am, there you may be also."
—JOHN 14:1-3, NRSV

Who can tell what will be the splendor and wonder of that reward, when at the Bar of Judgment the faithful are welcomed into the joy of the Lord? St. Augustine tries to find the words:

God will be the source of every satisfaction, more than any heart can rightly crave, more than life and health, food and wealth, glory and honor, peace and every good—so that God, as St Paul said, 'may be all in all.' He will be the consummation of all our desiring—the object of our unending vision, of our unlessening love, of our unwearying praise. And in this gift of vision, this response of love, this paean of praise, all alike will share, as all will share in everlasting life.[3]

But we must not think that we will be able to enjoy heaven or would even want to be there if we remain God's enemies in this life. If we do not change utterly, we shall never approach the joys of heaven. The holiness of God will be a terrifying and unbearable thing to us if we remain unrepentant. It would be better that the ground itself should open up and swallow us than to stand at the Great Bar as an enemy of God who hated his government and spat upon his covenant. Only the hell of endless separation from God remains for those who have chosen to be their own god. Wrongdoing will not end in the afterlife for those who oppose God. Hell is self-perpetuating. The rejection of God goes on in the rebel, and so does the punishment for this choice.

We should not think that those banished from the presence of God will somehow long to repent and turn to him in love. Such hatred merely grows. God has no choice but to leave those who despise him and his Son in the outer darkness of hell, for the door is locked from the inside. God forces no one into hell; people choose to be there, and ultimately God grants them their choice. Even in this, their freedom is not taken away.

How is it possible that a holy and just God can send people who have sinned to heaven? How can he allow them to come in? Only because of the love of Christ, for by his blood he has washed clean our guilty consciences. The great tragedy is that some people will force the hand of God through willful rebellion, and to them he will say "I never knew you; go away from me, you evildoers" (Matthew 7:23, NRSV).

HARVESTING HEAVEN

The seeds of heaven or hell are growing in us now. We are planting our vineyard for harvest in one state of being or another. We are either watering our knowledge of God in the plowed ground of a repentant heart, or we are leaving our hearts untended, the weeds of indifference springing up in the soil of a hardened soul.

> In the spiritual realm, heaven and hell are two opposite states of being. These states develop already now within each person's heart. We cannot see these two states of the soul any more than we can see the soul itself. But we can experience them just as clearly as we can feel physical pain or taste the delicious flavor of a sweet fruit.[4]

Only you and God know your own heart and the state in which you now live. The flavor of heaven is sweet, and if you have tasted it, you will know it. The bitterness of hell is acute and, like a stabbing pain, jars the soul. The harvest of hell is guilt, fear, restlessness, disappointment, resentment, hatred, and despair. But in heaven we reap delight. Its joy knows no end, its peace no passing, its pleasures no ceasing, its love no failing, its bliss no fading, for its God is everlasting.

Dear reader, invest your life in the treasures of heaven. Plant yourself in Christ Jesus. Whatever your failures or sin or state of soul, you will be transformed, and the unspeakable glories of heaven will be your reward.

Glorious things of thee are spoken,
Zion, city of our God!
He whose word cannot be broken
Formed thee for his own abode.
On the rock of ages founded,
What can shake thy sure repose?
With salvation's walls surrounded,
Thou mayest smile at all thy foes.

See! The streams of living waters,
Springing from eternal love,
Well supply thy sons and daughters,
And all fear of want remove;
Who can faint, whilst such a river
Ever flows their thirst to assuage?
Grace which, like the Lord, the Giver,
Never fails from age to age.

Saviour, if of Zion's city
I, through grace a member am,
Let the world deride or pity,
I will glory in thy name.
Fading is the worldling's pleasure,
All his boasted pomp and show,
Solid joys and lasting treasure
None but Zion's children know.
JOHN NEWTON (1725-1807)

Notes

Introduction

1. T. S. Eliot, "Choruses from the Rock."
2. Aldous Huxley, *Ends and Means* (London: Chatto & Windus, 1946), pp. 270, 273.
3. Matthew 6:21; Luke 12:34.
4. Proverbs 23:7, KJV.
5. Ecclesiastes 2:10-11, NIV.
6. Ecclesiastes 12:1, 8.
7. Quoted by Richard H. Seume, *Nehemiah: God's Builder* (Chicago: Moody Press, 1978), p. 19.
8. Jeremiah 29:13.

Preface

1. Ecclesiastes 12:12 (NRSV).
2. Jean-Paul Sartre and Simone de Beauvoir, "A Conversation About Death and God," *Harper's* magazine (February 1984), p. 39.
3. Blaise Pascal, *Pascal in a Nutshell* (Hodder and Stoughton, 1997), p. 48.
4. Ecclesiastes 3:6 (NLT).

Chapter 1: Look at That View!

1. British Parliamentary Committee, cited by Steve Wright, *Amazing but True* (Pocket Books, 1995), p. 215.
2. Socrates, cited by Robert Backhouse, *5,000 Quotations for Teachers and Preachers* (Kingsway Publications, 1994), p. 202.
3. Blaise Pascal, *Pascal in a Nutshell* (Hodder and Stoughton, 1997), p. 54.
4. C. S. Lewis, *God in the Dock* (William B. Eerdmans Publishing, 1970), pp. 101-102.
5. Matthew Parris, *The Times*.

Chapter 2: Beyond Reasonable Doubt

1. C. Stephen Evans, *Quest for Faith* (InterVarsity Press, 1986), p. 28.
2. *International Bulletin of Missionary Research* (January 1991), cited by John Blanchard, *Does God Believe in Atheists?* (Evangelical Press, 2000), p. 18.
3. *Daily Telegraph*, 16 December 1999.
4. E-mail from a friend, 1999; source unknown. For a detailed survey and exploration of belief in the existence of a supreme God in diverse cultures see Don Richardson, *Eternity in Their Hearts* (Regal Books, 1981).

5. Sir Arthur Conan Doyle, *The Penguin Complete Sherlock Holmes* (Penguin Books, 1981), p. 23.
6. Dr. Andrew Miller, in ed. R. J. Berry, *Real Science, Real Faith* (Monarch, 1991), pp. 94-95.
7. Blaise Pascal, *Pensées* (J. M. Dent & Sons Ltd, 1973, Everyman Library), p. 59.
8. Albert Einstein, personal correspondence to Queen Elizabeth of Belgium, 1932.
9. Pascal, *Pensées*, p. 101.
10. C. S. Lewis, *The Abolition of Man* (Fount Paperbacks, 1978), pp. 49-59.
11. Blaise Pascal, *Pascal in a Nutshell* (Hodder and Stoughton, 1997), pp. 66-67.

CHAPTER 3: THE SCIENCE OF BELIEF

1. Richard Dawkins, *The Selfish Gene* (Oxford University Press, 1976), p. 1.
2. Jonathan Leake, *The Sunday Times*, 9 September 2001.
3. Ibid.
4. Dr. Thomas Dwight, cited by John Ankerberg and John Weldon, *Darwin's Leap of Faith* (Harvest House, 1998), p. 110.
5. Karl R. Popper, cited by Professor Werner Gitt, *Did God Use Evolution?* (Christliche, 1993), p. 10.
6. Dr. Arno Penzias, cited by Ankerberg and Weldon, *Darwin's Leap of Faith*, p. 98.
7. Dr. Jonathan Sarfati, *Refuting Evolution* (Master Books, 1999), p. 16.
8. Boyce Rensberger, *How the World Works* (William Morrow, 1986), pp. 17-18.
9. Professor Richard Lewontin, "Billions and Billions of Demons," *The New York Review*, January 9, 1997, p. 31.
10. Dr. Arthur Custance, "Evolution: An Irrational Faith," in *Evolution or Creation?* Vol. 4, *The Doorway Papers* (Zondervan, 1976), pp. 173-174.

CHAPTER 4: FISH AND PHILOSOPHERS

1. Louis Agassiz, "Contribution to the Natural History of the United States," *American Journal of Science* (1860).
2. Richard Dawkins, *The Blind Watchmaker* (W. W. Norton, 1986), pp. 6-7.
3. *From the Life and Letters of Charles Darwin* (D. Appleton and Co., London), 2:400, note 1911.
4. Aldous Huxley, cited by John Ankerberg and John Weldon, *Darwin's Leap of Faith* (Harvest House, 1998).
5. Michael Denton, *Evolution—A Theory in Crisis* (Adler & Adler Publishers, 1986), p. 77.
6. Isaac Asimov, "In the Game of Energy and Thermodynamics You Can't Even Break Even," *Journal of the Smithsonian Institute* (June 1990), p. 6.
7. Professor Edward Nelson, cited by Ankerberg and Weldon, *Darwin's Leap of Faith*, p. 251.
8. Robert Oldershaw, "What's Wrong with the New Physics?" *New Scientist*, 22/29 December 1990.
9. Dr. Keith H. Wanser, in ed. Dr. John F. Ashton, *In Six Days* (New Holland Publishers, 2000), p. 93.
10. Ibid., p. 94.
11. David Wilkinson, *God, the Big Bang and Stephen Hawking* (Monarch Publications, 1996), p. 148.
12. Stephen Hawking, *A Brief History of Time* (Bantam Books, 1995), p. 13.

13. Professor Roger J. Gautheret, cited by Ankerberg and Weldon, *Darwin's Leap of Faith*, p. 268.
14. Charles Darwin, cited by Phillip E. Johnson, *Darwin on Trial* (InterVarsity Press, 1993), p. 103.
15. Dr. Stanley Miller, cited by J. Horgan, "In the Beginning . . ." *Scientific American*, February 1991.
16. Denton, *Evolution—A Theory in Crisis*, pp. 249-250.
17. Dr. Wilder-Smith, *The Natural Sciences Know Nothing of Evolution* (Master Books, 1981), p. 16.
18. Klaus Dose, "The Origin of Life: More Questions Than Answers," *Interdisciplinary Science Review 13*, 1988.
19. Dr. Walter L. Bradley, interview with Lee Strobel, *The Case for Faith* (Zondervan Publishing House, 2000), p. 141. When Dr. Bradley uses the phrase "Nobody still believes," he is not denying that some people still think chance can explain life; he is, however, suggesting that those informed on the subject, in his area of expertise, cannot accept, given the known facts, the notion of a purely random chance origin for life.
20. Ibid., p. 142.
21. Sir Francis Crick, *Life Itself* (Simon & Schuster, 1981).
22. Denton, *Evolution—A Theory in Crisis*, p. 250.
23. Dose, "The Origin of Life: More Questions Than Answers."
24. Dr. Howard Byington Holroyd, *Creation Research Society Quarterly*, June 1972, p. 5.
25. Charles Darwin, *The Origin of Species* (Wordsworth Editions Limited, 1998), p. 368.
26. Ibid., p. 213.
27. Ibid., p. 258.
28. William Dawson, cited by Ankerberg and Weldon, *Darwin's Leap of Faith*, p. 149.
29. Darwin, *The Origin of Species*, p. 214.
30. Denton, *Evolution—A Theory in Crisis*, pp. 160-161.
31. Ibid., p. 165.
32. Luther D. Sutherland, *Darwin's Enigma: Fossils and Other Problems* (Master Books, 1984), p. 88.
33. Stephen M. Stanley (Professor of Paleobiology, Johns Hopkins University), *Macroevolution: Pattern and Process* (W. H. Freeman & Co., 1979) p. 39.
34. Dr. George G. Simpson (leading paleontologist), *The Major Features of Evolution* (Columbia University Press, 1965), p. 360.
35. Denton, *Evolution—A Theory in Crisis*, p. 165.
36. Dr. Colin Patterson, cited by Sutherland, *Darwin's Enigma: Fossils and Other Problems*, p. 89.
37. Stephen Jay Gould, *Evolution Now: A Century After Darwin* (Macmillan, 1982), p. 140.
38. Denton, *Evolution—A Theory in Crisis*, pp. 165-166.
39. Simpson, *The Major Features of Evolution*, p. 263.
40. Denton, *Evolution—A Theory in Crisis*, pp. 193-194.
41. Ernest Mayr, *Populations, Species and Evolution* (Harvard University Press, 1970), p. 253.
42. Nils Heribert-Nilsson, *Synthetische Artbildung* (CWK Glerups, 1953), p. 11.
43. Ibid., pp. 1142-1143.

44. Charles Oxnard, *The Order of Man* (Yale University Press, 1984), cited by Dr. Jonathan Sarfati in *Refuting Evolution* (Master Books, 1999), p. 80. See pp. 79-89 for a fuller analysis.

45. For a fuller account of this remarkable story see Dr. Carl Wieland, "Brave Warriors with Words," *Creation Journal*, Vol. 23, No. 4 (September-November 2001), pp. 44-46.

46. Dr. Werner Gitt, *In the Beginning Was Information* (Christliche Literatur, 1997), p. 79.

47. Professor Paul Davies, cited by Alexander Williams, "Answers in Genesis," *Creation Journal*, Vol. 22, No. 2 (March-May, 2000), pp. 42-43. See also "Life Force," *New Scientist*, 163 (2204): 27-30 (18 September 1999).

48. Dr. Michael Behe, *Darwin's Black Box* (Touchstone Books, 1998), pp. 193ff.

49. Paul Kurtz, ed., *The Humanist Alternative* (Prometheus Books, 1973), p. 50.

50. Charles Darwin, *The Autobiography of Charles Darwin*, ed. Nora Barlow (W.W. Norton, 1958).

51. Sir Arthur Keith, *Evolution and Ethics* (G. P. Putnam's Sons, 1947), pp. 15, 71, 76.

52. Max Hocutt, "Toward an Ethic of Mutual Accommodation," in *Humanist Ethics*, ed. Morris B. Storer (Prometheus Books, 1980), p. 137.

53. Sir Julian Huxley, *The Stream of Life* (Watts & Co., 1926), p. 54.

54. Ibid., pp. 54-55.

55. Ibid., p. 55.

56. Ibid., p. 56.

57. Ibid.

58. Ibid.

59. Corliss Lamont, *The Philosophy of Humanism* (Frederick Ungar, 1982), p. 248.

60. Friedrich Von Bernhardi, cited in David A. Noebel, *Understanding the Times* (ACSI and Summit Ministries, 1995), p. 94.

61. Adam Sedgwick, cited in Ronald Clark, *The Survival of Charles Darwin* (Random House, 1984), p. 139.

62. Karl Marx, cited in Ankerberg and Weldon, *Darwin's Leap of Faith*, p. 35.

63. Keith, *Evolution and Ethics*, pp. 149-150.

64. Adolf Hitler, cited in Ankerberg and Weldon, *Darwin's Leap of Faith*, p. 33.

65. Adolf Hitler, *Mein Kampf* (Reynal and Hitchcock, 1940), pp. 397, 603, 406.

66. John P. Koster, Jr., *The Atheist Syndrome* (Wolgemuth & Hyatt, 1989), pp. 187-189.

67. Immanuel Kant, cited by John Blanchard, *Does God Believe in Atheists?* (Evangelical Press, 2000), p. 372.

68. C. S. Lewis, *God in the Dock* (William B. Eerdmans, 1972), p. 286.

CHAPTER 5: ECHOES OF EDEN

1. Ravi Zacharias, *Can Man Live Without God?* (Word Publishing, 1994).

2. Joe Kita, "Great House, Great Family, Great Car . . . Still Feel Miserable?" *Men's Health* (March 2001), pp. 101-102.

3. Sting, BBC Interview with Parkinson, 30 July 2001.

4. Blaise Pascal, *Pensées* (J. M. Dent & Sons, 1973), p. 22.

5. C. S. Lewis, *Mere Christianity* (Macmillan, 1952), p. 119.

6. Blaise Pascal, *Pascal in a Nutshell* (Hodder and Stoughton, 1997), p. 40.

7. Aldous Huxley, *Ends and Means* (Chatto & Windus, 1946), pp. 270, 273.

8. Augustine of Hippo, *Confessions*, Book 1, Section 1, Paragraph 1.

9. Pascal, *Pascal in a Nutshell*, p. 41.

CHAPTER 6: BIBLE BASHERS

1. Howard and Phyllis Rutledge and Mel and Lyla White, *In the Presence of Mine Enemies* (Fleming H. Revell, 1973).

2. Lord Denning, cited by Brian H. Edwards and Ian J. Shaw, *A.D.* (Day One Publications, 1999), p. 5.

3. *The Hadith*, Vol. 4, Nos. 830, 831, 832 and Vol. 5, Nos. 208, 209, 210, 211, and Vol. 6, Nos. 387, 388, 389, 390.

4. Author unknown.

5. Abraham Lincoln, cited by John Blanchard, *Does God Believe in Atheists?* (Evangelical Press, 2000), p. 412.

6. Robert Dick Wilson (former Professor of Semitic Philology, Princeton Theological Seminary), in ibid., p. 396.

7. Thomas Watson, *A Body of Divinity Contained in Sermons Upon the Westminster Assembly's Catechism* (The Banner of Truth Trust, 1958), p. 26. Original edition 1692.

8. Jean-Jacques Rousseau, cited by Josh McDowell and Don Stewart, *Answers to Tough Questions About the Christian Faith* (Alpha Books, 1997), p. 44.

9. Charles Dickens, cited by Stephen Gaukroger, *It Makes Sense* (Scripture Union, 1996), p. 52.

10. Gleason Archer, *Encyclopaedia of Bible Difficulties* (Zondervan Publishing House, 1982).

11. Theodore Roosevelt, cited by Robert Backhouse, *5,000 Quotations for Teachers and Preachers* (Kingsway Publications, 1994), p. 15.

12. Cicero, "De Divinations, 2.28," cited by V. Van der Loos in *The Miracle of Jesus* (E. J. Brill, 1965), p. 7.

13. C. S. Lewis, cited by John Young, *The Case Against Christ* (Hodder and Stoughton, 1994), p. 91.

14. Sir William Ramsay, *The Bearing of Recent Discovery on the Trustworthiness of the New Testament* (Baker Book House, 1953).

15. William F. Albright, cited in *The Answers Book*, ed. Dr. Don Batten (Answers in Genesis, 1999), p. 6. Cf. Josh McDowell, *Evidence That Demands a Verdict*, Vol. 1 (Authentic Publishing, 1998).

16. Nelson Glueck, *Rivers in the Desert* (Farrar, Strauss & Cudahy, 1959), p. 31.

17 John Calvin, cited in Graham Miller, *Calvin's Wisdom: An Anthology* (The Banner of Truth Trust, 1992), p. 25.

18. Frederick G. Kenyon, *The Bible and Archaeology* (Harper Brothers, 1940), p. 199.

CHAPTER 7: THE BIG STORY!

1. Richard Dawkins, *River Out of Eden: A Darwinian View of Life* (Basic Books/Harper Collins, 1995), pp. 132-133.

2. Claude Lanzmann, *Shoah: An Oral History of the Holocaust* (Pantheon Books, 1985), p. 30.

3. C. S. Lewis, *The Problem of Pain* (Macmillan, 1978), pp. 26-28.

4. Joanna Coles, interview of Ernest Gordon, "Savagery That Gave Me Faith," *The Times*, 6 August 2001.

5. Ibid.

6. Lewis, *The Problem of Pain*, p. 81ff.

7. St. Augustine, cited by Robert Backhouse, *5,000 Quotations for Teachers and Preachers* (Kingsway Publications, 1994), p. 208.

8. Lewis, *The Problem of Pain*, pp. 79-80.

9. Blaise Pascal, *Pensées* (J. M. Dent & Sons, 1973), pp. 65-66. (The quotation is in a more modern rendering.)
10. C. S. Lewis, *The Screwtape Letters* (Macmillan, 1982), p. 3.
11. John Donne, cited by David Porter, *The Monarch Book of Sins and Virtues* (Monarch Books, 1999), pp. 24-25.
12. Joan Collins, cited by J. John and Mark Stibbe, *A Box of Delights* (Monarch Books, 2001), p. 46.
13. Lewis, *The Problem of Pain*, p. 57.
14. Voltaire, cited by Robert Backhouse, *5,000 Quotations for Teachers and Preachers*, p. 152.
15. C. S. Lewis, *The Lion, the Witch and the Wardrobe* (HarperCollins, 1997), p. 148.

CHAPTER 8: THE LIBERATOR

1. H. G. Wells, cited in John Young, *The Case Against Christ* (Hodder & Stoughton, 1994), pp. 131-132.
2. Jean-Jacques Rousseau, cited by Tim LaHaye, *Jesus—Who Is He?* (Marshall Pickering, 1997), p. 40.
3. William Biederwolf, cited in John Blanchard, *Does God Believe in Atheists?* (Evangelical Press, 2000), p. 572.
4. Martin Luther, cited in Robert Backhouse, *5,000 Quotations for Teachers and Preachers* (Kingsway Publications, 1994), p. 28.
5. C. S. Lewis, *Mere Christianity* (Macmillan, 1952), pp. 55-56.
6. Ibid., pp. 56-57.
7. Socrates, cited in J. John, *Dead Sure* (InterVarsity Press, 1991).
8. Blaise Pascal, *Pensées* (J. M. Dent & Sons Ltd, 1973), p. 114.
9. Ravi Zacharias, *Jesus Among Other Gods* (Word Publishing, 2000), p. 91.

CHAPTER 9: A ROLLING STONE

1. Lord Darling, cited by Josh McDowell, *The Resurrection Factor* (Alpha Publications, 2001), p. 23.
2. Frank Morison, *Who Moved the Stone?* (Faber & Faber, 1958), pp. 102-103.
3. Sir Norman Anderson, *The Evidence for the Resurrection* (InterVarsity Press, 1988), pp. 6, 11.
4. Ibid., p. 15.
5. Simon Greenleaf, cited by Dr. Henry Morris, *Many Infallible Proofs* (Master Books, 2000), p. 105.
6. Stewart Henderson, "There Was No," in *Stand Up Poetry*, ed. Fraser Grace (Frameworks Publications, 1993), p. 33. Reproduced with the author's permission.

CHAPTER 10: THE GREAT BAR

1. Ravi Zacharias, *Cries of the Heart* (Word Publishing, 1998), p. 92.
2. Sundar Singh, *Wisdom of the Sadhu* (Plough Publishing, 2000), p. 170.
3. St. Augustine, *City of God* (Image Books, 1958), p. 541.
4. Singh, *Wisdom of the Sadhu*, p. 171.

index